CYBERNETICS

BEHAVIOURAL SCIENCES SERIES

General Editor P. McKellar, M.A., Ph.D., F.B.Ps.S., Professor and Head of the Department of Psychology, Otago University, New Zealand

A corner of the writer's cybernetics research laboratory at the University of Aston

CYBERNETICS

JOHN F. YOUNG, C.G.I.A., B.Sc., M.I.E.E., M.I.E.R.E.
Lecturer in Electronics, University of Aston, Birmingham

LONDON ILIFFE BOOKS LTD

NEW YORK AMERICAN ELSEVIER PUBLISHING COMPANY INC.

First published in 1969 by
Iliffe Books Ltd., 42 Russell Square, London, W.C.1

Published in U.S.A. by
American Elsevier Publishing Company, Inc.
52 Vanderbilt Avenue, New York, New York 10017

Library of Congress Catalog Card Number 69-14769

Printed in England

CONTENTS

PREFACE

It is unfortunate that many of the books on cybernetics which have been published fall into one of three categories. One type treats the reader as a moron who is to be astounded and so, it is hoped, impressed. Another treats the reader as though he were a potential employer who is to be baffled and so, it is hoped, impressed (and also, if possible, be made apprehensive and therefore generous). The third type of book includes the word 'cybernetics' in the title, but inside it apparently deals with an entirely different subject. It is hoped that the present book cannot be pigeon-holed into any of these categories.

A notable feature of cybernetics is the extent to which pseudo-mathematical tracts have appeared. Strangely, much of this writing has been produced not by mathematicians but by psychologists. Unfortunately, some of this 'mathematics' appears to be intended merely to impress and sometimes it has little relevance to any practical results which have been obtained. Possibly this is partly caused by the largely irrelevant mathematical chapters which Wiener inserted in his book on cybernetics. Whatever the reason, there has been a great deal of mathematical mumbo-jumbo associated with the subject. Fortunately, real mathematicians, physicists and engineers concerned with cybernetics have tended in general to be more restrained in their treatments. As a guide, it is suggested that the intending reader of any mathematical 'cybernetics' treatise should first search for any useful re-translation to plain language from symbols in the conclusions. If this cannot be produced, the mathematics is unlikely to be useful. When pressed, the people who have turned out some of these closely packed pages of symbols will sometimes even themselves express doubts about the relevance of their production. So much has been published in this field in recent years that no serious worker can afford the time to master any esoteric symbolisms and lengthy treatments merely to understand trivial and useless results.

Another astonishing thing about this field is the way in which various teams have worked along almost identical lines, each apparently acting as though no other teams existed. They announce

their own results in what appears to be a triumphant ignorance about other work. One can only suppose that perhaps this is the best way to get weighty financial backing for a research project.

The situation is by no means ideal, and there is a danger that cybernetics will become generally regarded as an up-to-date form of Black Magic, as a sort of twentieth century phrenology. If this unfortunately happens, then one whole field of research, at the border of many disciplines, will be robbed of the support it needs.

1968 J. F. Young

FOREWORD

The word *cybernetics* stems from the Ancient Greek. It was first used in modern times by Ampère in his *Essay on the Philosophy of the Sciences*, published in 1884. Following Norbert Wiener's important book of 1948, *Cybernetics, or Control and Communication in the Animal and the Machine*, this new discipline has had a distinctive influence on many branches of modern scientific thought. Today, cybernetics stands for an important area of research and development which, as John Young says, lies 'at the border of many disciplines'.

The thermostat and 'George', the automatic pilot of modern aviation, represent two standard examples of cybernetic machines. However, it is perhaps to the digital and analogue computers that we must look for some of the most striking examples of machine simulation of human functions. As late as 1952 there was only one computer in Britain. By 1956 there were 100, and it is estimated that by 1970 there will be 5,000. The author cites the estimate of Gordon Pask, a leading figure in the cybernetics field, that there are at present no fewer than 300 complex machines whose functioning reveals resemblances to those of living organisms. Perhaps Grey Walter's electronic tortoise ELMER is the best known of these, but there are others including, for example, Pask's SAKI, a teaching machine which, like a good human teacher, adjusts itself to the difficulties and rate of progress of the individual learner. Today, we have machines that perform maze-learning tasks like those mastered by the animals of the psychologist's laboratory. There are machines that simulate visual perception, pattern and shape recognition, and others that perform auditory tasks like speech recognition and response to the Morse code. A subject which began in the field of electronic engineering is serving to reorientate the specialist in many other fields.

As a University Lecturer in Electronics the author is an admirable guide to this important area of modern science. He is much concerned with the uses of cybernetics as a bridge between his own discipline and others, such as neuro-physiology, and both animal and human psychology. Moreover, he is able to draw not only on the achievements of laboratory research but also upon his own experience

of nearly two decades of working in industry. It is plain that both the Armed Forces and Industry have learned much, and still have more to learn, from cybernetic researches. In his account of the field the author presents several central ideas, of which two may be mentioned. First, that perhaps too much attention has been paid to the study of the 'learning' and 'remembering' functions of cybernetic machines: also very important is the study of simulations of the 'forgetting' process. Secondly, he places considerable emphasis upon the place of 'inhibition' in relation to the problems of simulating the higher human functions of 'intelligence' and 'thinking'. In this field cybernetics has had much to teach the psychologist preoccupied, as the psychologist has sometimes been, with the wrong kind of almost obsessive concern with 'objectivity'. Thus Turing, one important pioneer, did not hesitate to use introspection when necessary. From his study of his own thought processes while playing chess he evolved his complex chess machine, something he almost certainly would not have achieved had he confined himself purely to observation without such introspection.

The author is to be congratulated on his skilfully guided tour of the cybernetic field. He has, moreover, managed to cover a great deal that is of substance without the use of mathematics, and in lucid and non-technical language. For this we can be additionally grateful to him.

Peter McKellar
Series Editor

Department of Psychology,
Otago University,
Dunedin, New Zealand
1969

1

The Nervous System

Cybernetics was defined by Wiener as the study of communication and control in animal and machine. To discuss cybernetics adequately, we must first study animal, and in particular human animal, bodies and their systems of control. The human body contains many automatic defence mechanisms. For example, if a pointing finger is thrust towards your eye, then your eyelids immediately close in defence. This protective eye-blink is by no means an isolated example of automatic activity in the human body. If one's hand touches a hot plate, it is withdrawn rapidly and quite automatically, as is the foot which steps on a tack. In the early seventeenth century, René Descartes thought on such automatic activity and compared it with the automatic activity of a machine. He decided that the two are identical, that there is a direct cause and effect relationship which can explain all bodily activity. Descartes based his conclusions first on Harvey's demonstration of the hydraulic circulation of the blood in the body, secondly on his own observation of the similarity between the activity of animal bodies and the activity of the hydraulically-animated toys which were then fashionable in ornamental gardens, and, thirdly, on the observation that nerve cells are constructed in the form of long, narrow tubes. In fact, Descartes felt that the body must be controlled hydraulically by the pressure of fluid passed through the nerve tubes. We would not be tempted today to think of the control system of the body as hydraulic. Nevertheless, the writings of Descartes were valuable in that they popularised the idea of automatic bodily activity. Later, in England, the convenient term 'reflex action' was introduced to describe such activity.

In effect, Descartes regarded a living body as an automaton which obeys certain fixed rules of operation. He compared nerves with water-pipes, muscles with hydraulic engines, and the respiratory

system with a clock. In his *Discourse on Method*, Descartes suggested that it was possible to build a machine so like an ape 'or other irrational beast' that distinction between machine and animal would be impossible. He did not believe that an artificial man could be made because of the difficulties of building complex organs for speech and for reasoning. Prior to Descartes, it had been generally held that automatic motion, not directed by conscious thought, did not occur.

It seems obvious to us now that such automatic motion, such reflex action, must occur if an animal is to survive. If you took time to think about it when a finger was about to poke out your eye, you would be too late. Automatic action is vitally necessary. Let us consider further just what does happen in the case of the eye-blink reflex. A finger approaches the eye and the pattern of light falling on the retina changes (the retina is a mosaic of light-sensitive nerve cells at the back of the eye). The retina sends signals about this change back along the nerves to the brain. The signals are conveyed along the nerves electrically, and not hydraulically as Descartes thought. As soon as the electrical signals are received, the brain, without conscious thought, sends signals back along other nerves to the muscles which close the eyelids. The complete process is known as a reflex arc. It is quite automatic.

It will be seen from the above that the nerves play an important part in the reflex process. These are not the 'nerves' of popular present-day mythology, but the nerve fibres which exist in profusion in all living creatures. A nerve fibre is actually a single living cell, but it is a cell drawn out to a most unusual shape, as shown diagrammatically in Fig. 1. A single nerve fibre can be several feet long and yet only a very small fraction of an inch across. Bunches of these fibres connect remote parts of the body with the spinal cord which extends the length of the backbone. The spinal cord is itself made of nerve fibres. A signal starts along a nerve fibre as an electrical discharge across its outer tubular sheath. This electrical discharge affects neighbouring parts of the outer sheath which also then discharge. They in turn affect neighbouring parts and so the discharge propagates along the outer sheath of the long, thin cell rather in the way that a spark travels along the touchpaper of a firework. Walter has compared the action with a sort of electro-chemical smoke ring about 2 in. long travelling along the nerve. Quite high speeds of signal propagation are possible; 200 m.p.h. is not an uncommon signal speed in nerve fibres. This is why the reflex arcs such as the eye-blink are able to protect the body so rapidly.

In a reflex arc, some of the nerve fibres carry signals to the

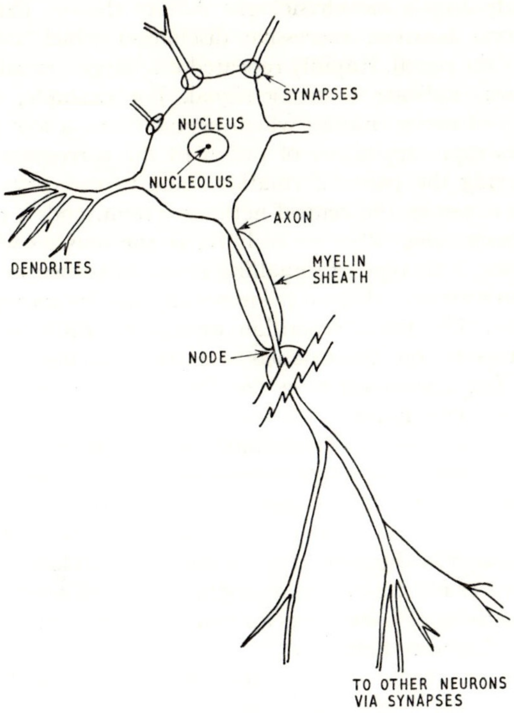

Fig. 1. Diagrammatic representation of a nerve cell

spinal cord or to the brain from, for example, the retina. These are called sensory fibres. Other fibres carry messages back from the central nervous system (spinal cord and brain) to the muscles. These are known as motor fibres. Both types of fibre operate in the same fashion, the only difference being in the direction of propagation of signals, either to or from the central nervous system formed by brain and spinal cord.

The nerve fibre passes signals on an all-or-nothing basis. Either the nerve sheath is conducting or it is not conducting, there is no in-between condition. How, then, does the nerve convey gradations of sensation or of movement? When the sheath conducts, it does so for a short time only, of the order of a thousandth of a second, and it then recovers to the non-conducting state. In effect, the signal which travels along the sheath of the nerve fibre passes any given point in a thousandth of a second or so. Shortly after the signal has passed a given point, the fibre is ready to repeat the performance.

In the early 1930's the physiologist Adrian showed that it is the time interval between successive discharges which conveys the intensity of the signal. Rapidly repeated discharges (usually referred to as pulses) indicate a strong signal. For example, the strong stimulation of nerve endings which occurs when a foot steps on a tack causes rapid repetition of pulses in the corresponding nerve fibres carrying the pain information back to the central nervous system. In response, the central nervous system sends a rapid train of pulses back along other nerve fibres to the muscles which withdraw the leg. This type of signalling is not unknown in radio and telecommunications, where it is known as pulse frequency modulation (PFM). The pulse repetition frequency (PRF) is varied in order to convey the instantaneous strength of the signal. Pulse repetition frequencies up to a few hundred per second are encountered in nerve fibres.

The whole activity of the animal nervous system is based on electrical discharges, although there is also a large basis of chemical activity which is gradually being understood. The electrical pulses in the nerve fibres can be detected by the use of electrical instruments, although in the early days of the study of electrical nervous activity very crude types of instrument had to be used. When the electrical activity is viewed on an instrument which can respond rapidly to electrical signals, it is possible to see the variation of pulse repetition frequency with the intensity of stimulation. The electrical activity is detected by attaching electrodes to the nerve cells and feeding the electrical signals from the electrodes to the instrument. As will be seen later, if the electrodes are attached to the scalp, then rhythmical electrical signals are picked up from the brain. This shows that the activity of the brain is at least partly electrical. The electrical rhythms of the brain are given various names depending on their rhythmical frequency. The commonest rhythm detected from the human brain is the alpha rhythm, in which the electrical signal repeats its rhythmical rising and falling between 8 and 13 times each second. On a machine called an electroencephalograph such electrical signals cause needles to deflect from side to side and to draw a trace on long strips of paper. The shape of the waves can then be studied in an attempt to obtain some clue as to how the brain works.

Let us leave the brain for a time and look instead at some of the features of nervous activity which have been revealed by making use of modern techniques of investigation. There are many types of nerve ending, each capable of detecting a different external phenomenon. Some nerve endings detect touch, some warmth, some light, some pain and so on. All of these different nerve endings are,

however, connected to nerve fibres which are similar in action, though there are several different forms and diameters of fibre. Those nerve endings which send back signals indicating that something is touching the arm are closely clustered around the small hairs on the arm. These hairs act as sensitive levers which help to activate the nerve endings. The fingerprint ridges probably have a similar levering effect on the underlying touch-nerve endings at the tips of the fingers. When such nerve endings are first touched there is a burst of electrical activity in the corresponding nerve fibres. Electrical pulses appear in the fibre. The repetition frequency of these pulses is at first high, perhaps 100 per second for a very strong pressure or 20 per second for a light pressure. However, if the pressure on the nerve endings is maintained constant, it is found that the pulse repetition frequency in the corresponding nerve becomes less, just as though the pressure on the nerve ending had decreased. The pulse repetition frequency falls to one half of its initial rate in about half a second, and after one second pulses are quite infrequent. If this process did not occur, our skin would be continuously irritated by the mere touch of our clothes. The phenomenon, which occurs in other types of nerve besides the touch nerves, is known as accommodation or adaptation. Adaptation ensures that changes of state produce a greater effect on the nervous system than do steady states. From a mathematical point of view this adaptation almost has the effect of differentiating the input signal, so that the pulse frequency modulated signal appearing in a touch nerve fibre depends more on the change of pressure than on the actual pressure.

As shown in Fig. 1, the nucleus of a nerve cell appears within one end of the fibre. This end is generally rather bulbous in shape, and smaller fibres known as dendrites coming, for example, from the sensitive nerve endings, terminate at its surface. Each dendrite forms a small knob almost touching the surface of the body of the nerve and separated from it only by an extremely thin barrier membrane. Such a junction is called a synapse. It seems that when an incoming dendrite is stimulated, its electrical signal causes a minute quantity of a chemical substance to be released, and this chemical can cross the barrier membrane and enter the body of the cell. There are often tens of thousands of synaptic junctions on a single nerve cell. When a sufficient number of these junctions is simultaneously stimulated by incoming dendrites, enough of the chemical substance is released to cause the cell to produce an electrical discharge across its surface membrane. It is this electrical discharge which propagates along the sheath of the nerve fibre to the far end, carrying information in an electrical form. At the far

end the fibre usually branches, the branches terminating at other nerve cell synapses or at muscles.

Some other points about the action at a synapse are of interest. The signals coming along the dendrites are all of a pulse, all-or-nothing form. However, the nerve cell summates these signals, and the repetition frequency of the impulses it produces depends on the total number of dendrites being stimulated simultaneously. Also, although the action appears to be chemical, the substance released at a synapse does not seem to persist, and summation is only effective if the various dendrites are stimulated within a few milliseconds of each other.

Not all of the dendrites have the effect of stimulation of the nerve cell. The signals from some dendrites tend instead to depress, or inhibit, the production of an outgoing discharge. As will be seen later, this inhibitory action is very important.

Nerve endings are not distributed evenly over the body. As an illustration of this, while two points touching the palm of the hand can be distinguished if they are more than about half an inch apart, on the back the two points cannot be distinguished from one if they are less than about 3 in. apart. This fact is generally taken to indicate that touch nerve endings are much closer together on the palm of the hand than on the back. The detection of changes and differences rather than absolute values is a feature of the nervous system. This feature leads to various illusions, optical and otherwise, but in general it ensures that the body is provided with the information which it needs to function satisfactorily without the necessity for great accuracy in the nervous system. A typical illusion produced by the dependence of perception on changes rather than on absolute values, is the well-known trick with three bowls of water. Place three bowls of water, one hot, one lukewarm and one cold, side by side. Then put one hand in the hot water and the other hand in the cold water. Leave your hands there for a short time so that the temperature-sensitive nerve endings become accustomed and adapted to the temperatures. Then suddenly plunge both hands into the bowl of lukewarm water. The lukewarm water seems hot to the hand which has been in cold water and yet it seems cold to the hand which has been in hot water. This is because the nerves signal the change of temperature, rather than the absolute value of the temperature, to the central nervous system.

Ernst Weber investigated this type of illusion in the first half of the nineteenth century, before modern measuring techniques could help him. He found that, if one compares two weights by holding them in the hands, and the difference in weight is just noticeable, then if both weights are increased, the difference must

also be increased in proportion if the two weights are still to be distinguishable. In other words, the difference of stimulus which can just be detected is proportional to the absolute value of the stimulus. This is known as Weber's law. Fechner elaborated Weber's law into the Weber–Fechner law. By thinking about the change of sensation corresponding to a given change of stimulus, Fechner arrived at a mathematical law of Nature: the magnitude of sensation increases arithmetically as the magnitude of the stimulus increases geometrically. An alternative way of stating this law is that the sensation is proportional to the logarithm of the magnitude of the stimulus. Fechner regarded this law as a mathematical statement of the relationship between body and mind. Later work showed that the law is often not followed at all accurately. However, Weber's law does give a picture of the general trend of the relationship between stimulus and sensation. That variation of stimulus which can just be detected is larger for a large stimulus than for a small stimulus.

Many of our senses can be duplicated by man-made devices. We are all familiar with telephones, radio and television, which makes use of artificial ears and eyes, and other senses are also duplicated in industrial equipment. One sense which has so far defied duplication or even scientific measurement is the sense of smell. This is an unfortunate fact since it has been suggested, by Orwell amongst others, that the sense of smell is frequently the basis of class and racial prejudice. At present it is not possible to determine scientifically whether or not the various classes and races really do smell differently or whether people who think so are being fooled by another bodily illusion. The smell (or olfactory) organ is rather a left-over from man's evolutionary development. While man has only one quarter of a square inch of olfactory nerve endings at the top of his nose, the dog has 10 sq. in. and the shark has 24 sq. ft.! One instance of the type of illusion created by the sense of smell is the taste of an onion. In actual fact, one is not able to tell the difference between the taste of a piece of onion and that of a piece of apple if one is blindfolded and one's nose is blocked.

Descartes believed that the body is purely reflex. Some of it is. For example, the internal organs of the body work incessantly, quite automatically absorbing oxygen from the air, digesting food, producing hormones. The heart beats automatically and we do not have to remember to instruct it to do so. However, the heart and other internal organs can vary in their action and their muscles are under the control of nerve fibres. There are sensory nerve endings inside the body, detecting what is happening and passing the information back to the central nervous system via the 'afferent'

nerve fibres. The central nervous system (brain and spinal cord) then passes back instructions to the internal muscles via the 'efferent' nerve fibres. The complete system of efferent nerve fibres going out from the central nervous system to the internal muscles is called the autonomic nervous system. The autonomic nervous system is actually formed from two separate systems of efferent fibres, known as the sympathetic system and the parasympathetic system. These two systems have purely reflex functions, intended to help the body to survive. If the central nervous system detects something in the external world which is to be feared, then the body must prepare either for flight or to fight. In either case, the pulsing of the heart must become quicker and stronger to give a quicker blood flow to the muscles and the rest of the body, the lungs must prepare to take in extra oxygen, and so on.

These functions are performed by the sympathetic nervous system quite automatically on receipt of the 'fear' signal from the central nervous system. There is a very long list of these reflex 'fear' reactions caused by the sympathetic nervous system. Some of the reactions have been used to advantage by interrogators to detect fear. For example, activation of the sympathetic nervous system causes the iris of the eye to dilate or increase in size just as though less light was falling on the eye. Fear can make the mouth go dry. This has been used by witch-doctors to find the guilty party from a number of suspects. All the suspects are made to put a pebble in their mouths for a short time. The suspect with the dry pebble is then the unfortunate one.

While the sympathetic nervous system appears to be adapted to prepare the body for a fight, the other component of the autonomic system, the parasympathetic nerves, seems to be adapted to restore the body after violent activity is over. Those blood vessels previously constricted by the sympathetic nervous system are dilated by the parasympathetic system and vice versa. The heart rate is reduced and the bronchioles of the lungs are contracted by the parasympathetic system when the danger is over.

The functions of the autonomic nervous system which have been discussed here are extreme examples of the prime function. The autonomic system appears to exist mainly in order to maintain constant conditions in the interior of the body. The sympathetic nervous system, for example, regulates the temperature of the body by controlling the size of the blood vessels near the surface of the skin. Such a regulating process is quite well known in man-made machines, and we can therefore make use of the concepts and language used by engineers to discuss the operation of such machines in order to facilitate description of the regulating action of the

autonomic nervous system of the body. In the example just considered, the nervous system of the body acts in the same basic way as a man-made thermostat, though the components of the two systems are naturally very different. The central nervous system can easily send signals to the muscles of the skin blood vessels in order to dilate them, increase the skin blood flow and so raise the skin temperature. However, the central nervous system must be capable of determining when and by how much to increase or to decrease the blood flow if the temperature of the body falls or rises. This information is obtained from the temperature-sensitive nerve endings in the body. These act as measuring devices which feed back temperature information over the nerve fibres to the central nervous system if the body temperature is incorrect.

Such an arrangement possesses all the features of information 'feedback' which is used in many different forms of man-made 'closed-loop regulators'. They are called closed-loop regulators or control systems because the information flows around a closed loop of information-carrying arrangements. Information about the temperature flows from the temperature sensor to the control system, which changes the conditions in such a way as to correct the temperature. The corrections are detected by the temperature sensor which feeds back information to the control system and so on. The information flows around a closed system. Most of the nervous control of the body is arranged in this way, not only the mainly regulatory action of the autonomic nervous system. The nervous system controls muscles which operate on the environment of the body. Information on the environment is then fed back to the central nervous system via nerve endings and nerve fibres. For example, if you are cold and your autonomic system has not succeeded in raising your temperature sufficiently, you can switch on an electric fire. Your hand is guided to the switch by your muscles acting on signals coming from the central nervous system, which in turn is acting on signals from the nerve endings in the retina of your eye. The signals from the retina could be feeding back information about the deviation of the actual position of your hand from the desired position, and the central nervous system would be controlling the muscles accordingly. The loop of information flow is again closed, in this case via your environment, the external world.

It is interesting to notice here that since the time of Descartes, scientists have attempted to explain the actions of the body by comparison with the actions of engineering devices current in their own time. This process still continues, and in some respects today, as always in the past, engineers are attempting to explain the actions of their machines in terms of bodily actions. Encouragement of such

a reciprocal flow of information is the real function of the branch of science which Wiener has called 'cybernetics'. Like all other studies at the borderline between related fields of knowledge, it is likely to bring real scientific progress.

In the early 1930's, engineers and scientists were beginning to account successfully for some of the puzzling features of the behaviour of their closed-loop feedback machines. At the same time biologists were investigating some of the closed-loop behaviour of animal organisms. Cannon introduced the term 'homeostasis' to describe the action of the body in controlling itself and its environment in order to provide suitable conditions for continued existence. The concept of homeostasis has more recently been elaborated by Ashby, who has attempted to produce quasi-mathematical theories of the action of the central nervous system.

2

Reflexes, Inhibition and Survival

The internal autonomic system appears to act in a purely reflex manner. Many activities of lower forms of life seem at first sight to be purely reflex, and such activities have been catalogued and systematically named. The roots of these names are -tropism (turning of the body) and -taxis (movement of the body), and the action can be either positive or negative. For example, positive phototropism means a turning towards light, while negative thermotaxis means a movement away from heat. These activities are not infallible, and this indicates that some complexity is involved and that the actions are not purely reflex. It should be noted that tropism and taxis refer to movement of the whole body, while in general the term reflex action is applied to the activity of a part only of the body. Although Descartes thought that all animal and human activity could be explained in terms of simple reflex action, this view makes no allowance for another basic feature of animal activity, namely learning from experience.

If all animal activity was purely reflex, then no animal would be capable of learning from its experience. An animal would only be able to make a given fixed reaction to any particular set of circumstances even if this reaction had previously produced unfortunate results. Feedback is a part of much reflex activity and, while it accounts for the control of the degree of action, it alone cannot account for the phenomenon of learning. Adaptation is a feature of nervous activity but it cannot account for learning. Although progress has been and is being made in investigations into the details of the actual mechanism of learning, no completely satisfactory explanation is as yet forthcoming. At the present stage, because of the complexity of nervous activity when learning is considered, we have to fall back on a study of behaviour rather than a study of mechanism. Instead of attempting to find the actual

nervous pathways responsible for complex animal behaviour, we study the behaviour itself and try to discover underlying patterns. These patterns might then eventually give us a clue as to the responsible mechanism to look for in the central nervous system. We must leave physiology and resort to psychology. However, this need not stop us from using the engineering language of feedback systems where it might lead to useful concepts.

It is a very old idea that much learning (some would say all learning) is based on association of ideas. Good teachers certainly rely on this fact, by making sure that every new concept which is introduced has some relationship to another concept which is already familiar to the student. The new concept is then learned by association with the old. If the nervous system is studied, it is found that one reflex can become associated with another. The physiologist Pavlov, carrying out an investigation into reasons for the secretion of saliva in the mouth, was led to an experimental study of association. He has stated that he started to record all the external stimuli falling on the animal at the time that its reflex reaction (the secretion of saliva) was manifested, at the same time recording all changes in the reaction of the animal. Pavlov found that it was quite possible to demonstrate the association of one reflex with another. As an example, he found that if he presented food to a dog, naturally enough the sight of the food made the animal's mouth water in preparation for eating. This is a natural, built-in reflex. However, Pavlov found that if he rang a bell each time that he presented the food, then the animal came to associate the bell with food. After repeating the performance a sufficient number of times, it was possible to make the animal's mouth water simply by ringing the bell without presenting food at all. The sound of the bell, acting on the nerve endings in the ear of the dog, became so closely associated with food that it was possible for the signals from the ear alone to cause the central nervous system to send signals along nerve fibres to the mouth to cause saliva to flow. In effect, Pavlov found that it was possible to establish a completely new, learned, reflex by association with a natural, built-in reflex. From a number of possible names for such learned reflexes, Pavlov chose the name 'conditioned reflex' and he then referred to the built-in type of reflex as 'unconditioned'. This latter term is rather unfortunate since it can seem to suggest that a built-in reflex is somewhat incomplete. Pavlov himself suggested alternative names, but the term 'conditioned reflex' is now so widely adopted that it would be unwise at this stage to use any other term.

Pavlov started from Descartes' conception of reflex action of the body. We have seen earlier that straightforward reflex action is

inflexible and it cannot be used to explain how an animal learns. However, add to Descartes' ideas the conditioning processes of reflexes and learning can be explained. In the example quoted, it can be said that the animal learns to associate the sound of the bell with food. At one time it appeared that this learning or conditioning behaviour operated via the brain, and that although an animal was still capable of fairly complex movement after removal of the brain, it was not capable of further learning. Pavlov believed this and so did the great physiologist Sherrington. Today, however, it is beginning to seem less certain that the brain always plays an essential part in the learning process. Experimental effects are often clouded by the severe shock to the animal organism resulting from the operation of cutting the spinal cord or of complete removal of the brain. Certainly, after the spinal cord has been cut the shock to the system is such that the body shows no response whatever to stimulation below the cut; even simple reflexes are absent. It is found that later the body recovers and reflexes return, though sensation does not and conditioning is non-existent. The shock to the organism is severe and this shock can affect subsequent activity. In recent years various workers have shown that co-ordinated activity in the cat is still possible after the spinal cord has been cut. In some cases such animals have, with patience, been trained to walk. Such work has been described by Shurrager (1950). At the present time it would appear that the view of physiologists is that all parts of the central nervous system take part in some learning at least and that such learning is not exclusive to the brain. Even so, it seems to be generally agreed that where complex learning is involved, the brain must play its part.

Not all of the nervous system can be conditioned. In particular, the individual reflex arcs of the autonomic nervous system apparently continue to work consistently without modification of the built-in method of operation by conditioning, although the autonomic system as a whole is under central control. Here there are minor closed-loop control systems such as that controlling the pupil of the eye. If the retina detects an increased amount of light, signals are sent to the central nervous system which in turn sends back signals to the iris muscles which cause the pupil to contract and so restore the amount of light falling on the retina to a reasonable quantity. This reflex is not under mental control, it is completely automatic and one is not conscious that it has occurred. The watering of the mouth which occurs when one smells food is not under mental control, but one is conscious that it has happened. Some reflexes can be regarded as partly voluntary in that they can be controlled mentally, although this is not usually done. Typical of

these is the protective eye-blink which has been discussed previously. When an object approaches the eye, the lid closes involuntarily. However, it is possible by the exertion of will-power to prevent the eye from closing, particularly if the object has several times previously approached the eye without touching it. We say that the blink can be inhibited. In addition to the three types of action mentioned, there are also purely voluntary actions and some actions which are sometimes voluntary and sometimes reflex. As Haldane and Huxley have pointed out, only an experienced schoolmaster can tell voluntary from reflex coughing.

The new factor which has been mentioned above is inhibition. Descartes postulated the occurrence of inhibition, though this was not demonstrated experimentally until more than 200 years after his suggestion. Descartes guessed correctly that there must be two sets of muscles moving the eye from side to side, one set relaxing as the other set contracts. Wherever two muscles act in opposition, it is necessary that the contraction of one be inhibited when the other one contracts, since otherwise there would be no nett movement. It is pretty clear from experimental results that in general this inhibition results from the action of the central nervous system. Often a muscle will receive one inhibitor nerve fibre for every two or three excitor fibres.

In some cases one of the autonomic nervous systems excites muscular activity while the other system inhibits it. For example, the parasympathetic nervous system can inhibit the beating of the heart, while the sympathetic nervous system has the opposing effect of acceleration. It was in the latter half of the nineteenth century that experimental evidence for the existence of inhibition began to accumulate. Nerve fibres having an inhibitory action on muscles were found and the contraction and inhibition of opposing muscles was demonstrated. Later, Sherrington demonstrated that inhibition could occur at junctions between nerves in the central nervous system. Some reflexes can be inhibited for several seconds by an impulse entering the corresponding region of the spinal cord via another nerve fibre. To illustrate this, we can consider the knee-jerk reflex. This is a well-known reflex which is used to test the state of the nervous system of a patient. The patient sits down with legs crossed, one knee over the other. A light tap just below his kneecap will then cause the muscle in his leg to twitch and the leg to straighten momentarily. The usefulness of this test lies in its variability. If there is anything wrong with the central nervous system, variations of the knee-jerk reflex can indicate the fact to a trained eye. It is found however, that a slight pinprick in the foot can inhibit the knee-jerk reflex for several seconds. The signals from the nerves affected by the

pinprick enter the spinal region and there cause inhibition of signals coming later from the knee, preventing for a short time the signals from being returned to the leg muscles to initiate the twitch.

The inhibition of the knee-jerk due to a pinprick is involuntary. The inhibition of the eye-blink is voluntary. It is possible for conditioned inhibition to be set up in the same way that conditioned reflexes are formed. In particular, an acquired conditioned reflex can be inhibited by an external disturbance. For example, if a bell rings nearly every time that food is presented to a dog, the bell alone can eventually cause the dog's mouth to water in anticipation. However, if sometimes a lamp flashes at the same time as the bell rings, and on these occasions no food is presented to the dog, the lamp will eventually inhibit the acquired reflex whenever it shines. The study of inhibitioning as applied to reflexes can become very complicated, as will be seen from the example quoted. Work is currently being carried out on this aspect of nervous activity. Typical of this is the recent demonstration by Ratcliff that the electrical pulses sent from a single nerve cell in the eye of a crab whenever the cell is illuminated, can be partly inhibited when nearby nerve cells are also illuminated at the same time. It is possible that this inhibitory process in the eye of a crab helps to emphasise the contrast between light and dark patches in the visual pattern perceived by the creature.

Like natural and conditioned reflex action, inhibition has homeostasis as its ultimate object. Pavlov put the point that an animal must respond to changes in its environment in such a manner that its responsive activity is directed towards the preservation of its existence. It is as well when thinking about such things to be quite sure about what we mean by 'existence'. It seems clear that Pavlov meant 'life'. J. Z. Young has pointed out that a characteristic of living organisms is that they hold themselves distinct and separate from their surroundings. And yet on a molecular scale they are in a state of constant interchange with their surroundings. Studies using radioactive isotopes have shown that even the bones of the body are not composed of the same atoms permanently, but only retain particular atoms for a limited time. Thus although a living body maintains itself distinct from its surroundings, it does this by taking atoms and molecules from the surroundings and organising them into a living shape. Mathematically, this characteristic of life can be called negative entropy. The entropy of any system increases as it becomes more disorganised, decreases as it becomes more organised. A deck of cards with all the suits and numbers in order has low entropy. Shuffle the cards and the entropy increases. Throw the deck in the air so that the cards spread

randomly all around the room and the entropy increases still more. Collect all the cards together and sort them into suits and correct number order and the entropy is decreased to its original value. Living organisms all have the property of taking up randomly distributed matter and organising it into a logical, living shape. When this process of organisation ceases, the organism can no longer be said to be alive.

Thus the primary aim of life appears to be to maintain its state of organisation and to interchange atoms and molecules with its surroundings in the process. As an example, animals tend to lose water by evaporation and excretion, but each animal is capable of detecting water in its surroundings and of taking it up to replace losses. The nervous system detects changes or the possibility of changes of the organisation, and it operates muscles in order to change the environment (possibly by moving to a new environment) to maintain the state of organisation unchanged. Information about the resulting state is fed back to the central nervous system via the sensory nerve fibres, and this process continues until the environment is suitable for the continued existence of the animal organism.

A certain amount of the information about how to react to various environmental conditions in order to restore the required state is built-in in the form of nerve fibres in definite pathways. These are the reflex nerve fibres, and the resulting behaviour pattern we call instinctive behaviour. A chicken when first hatched will peck at any bright object or mark. In some cases it is successful and it finds food. In other cases it merely pecks an object which must not be eaten and is consequently rejected, or else it pecks nothing at all. Such instinctive behaviour is quite reflex, and it serves to keep the chicken alive when it is small. However, the chicken soon learns to associate the visual stimuli with 'food' or 'non-food' and to peck more selectively. In this way the chicken maintains its internal organisation and differentiates itself from its environment.

So far we have only considered the action of the nerves, and the notion of the central nervous system has been deliberately kept vague. The central nervous system is that part of the nervous system to which sensory nerve endings send signals via their nerve fibres and from which nerve fibres carry signals to muscles. In effect, the central nervous system is a telephone exchange in which it is determined which muscles shall be energised in response to signals from which sensory nerve endings. In the lower forms of life, the central nervous system is little more than a junction between numbers of nerve fibres. However, as we move up the tree of evolution, in more advanced forms of life we find that there is a lengthy region in which nerve fibres meet. This is the site for a

richer interplay between nerve impulses, the site in which conditioning of reflexes and of inhibitions can take place. In still higher forms of life there appears at one end of this lengthy 'spinal cord' region a bulge, the first rudiments of the brain. This bulging region seems to provide the site for an even more complex interchange of nervous impulses. As we progress along the evolutionary chain, the brain becomes more complex and its action even more difficult to follow. At present at the top of the evolutionary tree is man, apparently the first creature to realise that he possesses a brain and nervous system, longing to know how and why he behaves as he does. Can the possessor of a brain eventually understand how that brain works? We must work on the assumption that he can, unless we can produce scientific proof that such a thing is impossible. The road to understanding may be long and hard, but it must be followed if we are to continue scientific progress.

Instinctive behaviour is purely reflex behaviour which helps the living creature to survive in its normal environment. Like the shape of the creature, the instincts have appeared over the ages by a process of natural selection. Those creatures born with certain reflexes survived longer and better in a particular environment than creatures born without these reflexes. The creatures having the reflexes therefore had a greater opportunity to grow to maturity and to reproduce and so perpetuate the reflexes appropriate to the environment. The whole collection of built-in, inborn reflexes forms the instincts of the creature. The instincts are all-important to survival in the lower forms of life, but as the nervous system evolved instincts became less important in the adult creature. The newly-born creature must of necessity rely on its instincts to guide its actions, but as it grows, provided that it has a capable central nervous system, the creature can rely more and more on acquired, conditioned reflexes and inhibitions.

In effect, reproduction is one part of survival. How else can organisms adapt themselves to the gradual but drastic long-term changes of environment which are bound to occur? An organism which lived for ever would only be successful in an unchanging environment, and an unchanging environment does not seem to be the way of Nature. So there are the changes in body and in nervous system over the generations due to the fact that evolution is taking care of long-term adaptation to the environment, while there is the conditioning of reflexes and of inhibitions taking care of short-term adaptation. The whole operation is directed to one end—survival of the organism, differentiated from but interchanging molecules with its environment. During the life span of an individual, it fights entropy and collects together randomly distributed bits and organ-

ises them into a whole. But eventually the organism will lose the fight and its entropy will increase. It will become disorganised as its body breaks up into randomly distributed molecules. However, by this time it will with any luck have reproduced and reared its young to maturity. It seems that in Nature's view this is survival. The possibility of simply regenerating a complete organism in the same way that some animals regenerate lost limbs appears not to appeal to Nature yet, perhaps because such a process would not give sufficient opportunity for adaptation to long-term changes of environment.

3

The Brain

Interesting as is the evolutionary aspect of survival, we are concerned here with the short-term view. The nervous system, including its highest development, the brain, is concerned with day-to-day survival of an individual organism. Instinctive behaviour must enter into everyday living, particularly so far as producing and caring for the young are concerned. This is the organism ensuring long-term survival. However, purely instinctive behaviour tends to become concealed by the rich patchwork of acquired conditioned behaviour, particularly in the higher creatures. The drive is always for survival of the organism. No hint of altruism here! The organism is inherently selfish. It is only concerned with the survival of itself and its young. To a certain extent, since the existence of like organisms helps to perpetuate the race, one might expect the instincts to drive an organism to help like organisms to survive. If such a drive exists, it is the herd instinct. Is there any other reason why an organism should be altruistic?

Only the higher forms of life have any spark of what might be called altruism. Let us, then, investigate the features of the nervous system to see what distinguishes higher from lower forms of life, in the hope that we may discover the reasons for and the mode of action of this so-called altruism. The outstanding feature which is noticed, as one scans upward along the evolutionary scale, is the growing importance of inhibition in the nervous system. It begins merely as a reciprocal action, as in the autonomic nervous system. Because the same types of nerve fibres are used for inhibition as for excitation of reflexes, conditioning of inhibition is quite possible as mentioned earlier. The organism can learn to inhibit reflexes where this proves advantageous to survival in the existing environment. Thus, in effect, an instinctive reflex action is held off when some

disturbance is present until the time is more opportune for indulgence of the reflex.

Most animals will pull food towards them if they are restrained from moving towards the food. This is an instinctive action. If there is an obstacle in the way of the food, many animals are lost. They will simply continue to try in a reflex fashion to drag the food towards them despite the obstacle. Higher forms of animals, for example monkeys, can inhibit the dragging action and can first push the food away from them in order to guide it around the obstacle before pulling it towards them. What insight! What intelligence! Is it possible that all intelligence resides merely in a capacity for inhibition of reflex activity until the occurrence of an opportune moment for the reflex to be allowed to proceed? In his book *The Human Brain*, Lassek pointed out that early forms of man had to learn simultaneously to lower the threshold of excitability to those stimuli which could assist him in advancing, and to block those which might do him harm and retard his progress.

If the brains of animals at various levels of evolution are compared, one outstanding feature is noticed. There seems to be some connection between the size and, more particularly, the shape of the brain of different types of animal and the complexity of their activity. In lower forms of life the brain is merely a forward extension of the central nervous system and it appears to be devoted almost entirely to association of the sense of smell with other sensory inputs. This is not surprising when one considers the importance of the sense of smell to the survival of such creatures. As evolution proceeded and fish began to crawl from the sea, the smell, or olfactory, centre of the nervous system expanded. Perhaps the difference between the senses of taste and smell should be cleared up at this point, since the question of the difference is a very real one when the activity of fish is considered. The sense of smell detects minute particles coming from a distance and so enables the nervous system to cause an organism to move in an appropriate direction. On the other hand, the nerve endings concerned with taste are inactive until they are actually touched by an object. The olfactory nerves are concerned with detection at a distance, while the taste nerves are concerned with purely local detection. While movement of the organism is likely to be initiated depending on the information obtained from the olfactory nerves, the information from taste nerves merely indicates to the central nervous system whether something should be eaten or rejected.

In the fish, nerve fibres from the nose can be found in all parts of the central nervous system. However, amphibian animals have parts of the brain which do not appear to be associated directly with the

sense of smell at all. The sense of sight has an increasing importance, as has the sense of hearing. In the amphibia, the olfactory lobes are only slightly smaller than the rest of the brain, that part usually called the forebrain. In a reptile such as an alligator, however, it is found that the forebrain is appreciably larger than the olfactory lobes. The alligator spends much of its time out of the water and it is capable of catching animals, such as pigs, on land. In a bird such as a pigeon, the forebrain is very much, say ten times, larger than the now small olfactory lobes. It seems that as, in the course of evolution, animals moved higher and higher from the level of the sea, they found less and less need for the sense of smell. For example, if the brain of a jumping shrew (which lives on the ground) is compared with that of a tree shrew, it is found that the latter has a smaller olfactory lobe but a larger visual region than the former.

As we progress still higher up the family tree of evolution, the forebrain becomes larger while the outside of the forebrain (the cerebrum) becomes crinkled and fissured. This was noted in the fifth century B.C. by Erasistratus, who suggested a correlation between intellectual capacity and the amount of fissuring of the cerebrum. It has been suggested that the reason for this fissuring might be that while the volume of the brain varies as the cube of the linear dimensions, the surface area only varies as the square of the linear dimensions. Consequently, if the circumference of the brain doubles, there is a tendency for its volume to increase eight times while its surface area is only multiplied by four. Now the surface of the brain is quite important, in fact it is so important that it has a special name—the cortex. Strictly speaking, this term applies to the outer covering of anything, since it is derived from the Latin term for 'bark', but it is today taken as mainly applying to the extensively studied outer layer of the brain. As the size of the brain has increased through evolution, there has tended to be an imbalance between the amount of surface layer and the amount of interior. The balance is to some extent restored by the fissuring of the surface, which has the effect of increasing the surface area without increasing the volume. The fissuring also brings various parts of the cortex nearer together and so provides greater opportunity for interconnection between the nerve cells and fibres of the cortex. When fissuring first appeared in the evolutionary chain, it was mainly simple fissuring from front to back of the cortex. In still higher animals the volume of the brain increased even more and cross-fissures appeared in the cerebrum. In man, cerebral fissures run in all directions, so that the surface area of the human brain is fifteen times that of the monkey. Is it possible that this simple fact of the relationship between linear dimension, area and volume places a limit on the evolution of brain

as we know it? Our descendants will know the answer, though some scientists think now that fissuring of the brain has nothing to do with mental ability. The whale is quoted as an example of an extremely fissured brain not accompanied by evidence of outstanding mental ability, as is the dolphin! The fissuring of the surface of the brain also serves to assist the blood supply to the cortex.

In the spinal column the nerve fibres are on the outside of a tube. Inside the tube is a central H-section core of so-called grey matter which appears to provide for interconnections between the nerve fibres running along the outside of the tube. The exterior nerve fibres are referred to collectively as the 'white matter' because, when a cross-section of the spinal cord is taken, it is the whiteness of the sheath of nerve fibres which differentiates them from the H-shaped central grey core. In the brain the positions of grey matter and white matter are reversed. The cortex is a layer of grey, sheathless, nerve cells about one-eighth of an inch thick on the outside of the cerebrum, the inside of which is white.

Electrical techniques have made it possible to identify various regions of the cortex. Indeed, some regions were identified long before electrical techniques were available. Early studies of human anatomy had revealed that the brain surface was fissured, and as such studies progressed certain standard features became obvious. All human brains are divided by a deep longitudinal fissure into two roughly equal halves. Three other quite large fissures appear in the brains of monkeys and of man, as shown in Fig. 2. One, the Rolandic

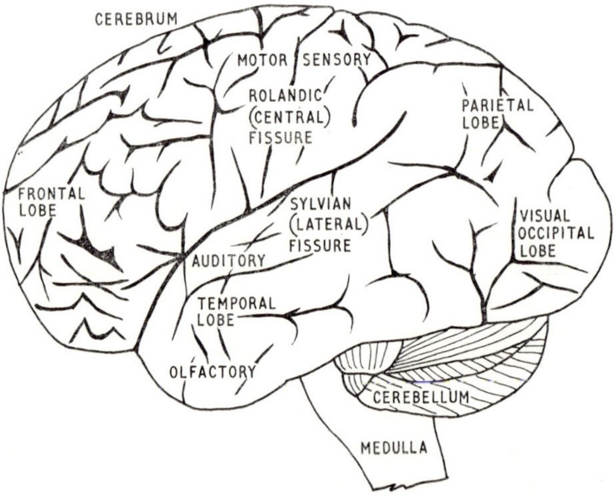

Fig. 2. The human brain

fissure, runs across the top of the brain, almost from ear to ear. The other two are the Sylvian fissures, one on either side of the brain running backwards and upwards over the ears. These large fissures divide the brain into regions which are quite easily recognisable. The regions were in the main named after the portion of the skull which covered them. Thus the rear parts of the brain, under the occipital bones of the skull, are known as the occipital lobes of the brain. Above and in front of the occipital lobes are the parietal lobes, under the parietal bone of the skull. The regions right at the front of the cerebrum are known as the frontal lobes.

Although Willis suggested in the early seventeenth century that the brain is the part of the body responsible for thought, this did not stimulate much work on the brain at the time. In fact, it had all been said and ignored before in the fifth century B.C. by that great man of medicine, Hippocrates. In an oft-quoted passage, Hippocrates said 'Man ought to know that from the brain and from the brain only, arise our pleasures, joys, laughter and jests as well as our sorrows, pains, griefs and tears. Through it, in particular, we think, see, hear and distinguish the ugly from the beautiful, the bad from the good, the pleasant from the unpleasant. It is the same thing which makes us mad and delirious, inspires us with dread and fear, whether by night or by day, brings sleeplessness, inopportune mistakes, aimless anxieties, absent-mindedness and acts that are contrary to habit. These things which we suffer all come from the brain when it is not healthy. . . .'

Hippocrates had noted that a blow on one side of the head could produce paralysis of the opposite side of the body. Over twenty-one centuries later, in the early eighteenth century, Petit suggested that each half of the brain controls movement on the opposite side of the body. Later, von Haller insisted that all parts of the brain act equally and the brain functions as a whole. If one part of the brain is injured, another region takes over the duties of the injured part. In effect, this denies any localisation of brain activity. Von Haller based his conclusions on a certain amount of experimental work on animals. Such work continues today, for example Sperry has described the work at the California Institute of Technology, but no very clear conclusion is apparent.

In the absence of thorough scientific work on the brain, the world welcomed the phrenology of Gall which appeared early in the nineteenth century. This assumed that emotions were extremely localised in the brain and that they could be detected by the bumps on the skull. Because of the clairvoyant nature of this so-called science of phrenology, Gall is not regarded highly by many scientists. However, Gall actually did some very good work on the localisation

of cortex activity, and he revealed the nature of the grey and white matter of the brain. He contributed to the knowledge of the pathways followed by nerve fibres in the brain, and he suggested the reason for the fissuring of the cerebrum discussed above.

Above all, Gall provided a framework of anatomical knowledge about the brain on which the physiologists could build. By removal of the brains of animals, Flourens demonstrated that the brain is concerned with thought and control. Clive Bell carried out experiments on the spinal cords of animals and found out that the motor fibres are in front and the sensory fibres behind. Following Willis, Gennari had noted a well-marked white line in the occipital region of the cortex. This region was later confirmed by Baillarger, and we now know that it is the visual cortex, that part of the cortex most concerned with seeing. Baillarger was also able to show that the nerve cells of the cortex form six fairly well-defined layers. Andral, Bouillaud and Dax all studied cases in which there had been damage to the brain, and all three found that there was some evidence for the existence of a region on the left side of the brain which controls the power of speech. Dax in particular collected evidence of over one hundred human cases.

All this work early in the nineteenth century laid the foundation for the important work done in the middle of the century. On the rather inadequate evidence of only two autopsies on patients who had been paralysed on the right side and who had also lost their power of speech, Broca concluded that speech control was localised in a small area of the left frontal lobe. He was right. The region is now called Broca's area. Only a few years later, Hughlings Jackson came to the conclusion that there was an even more significant localisation of function in the brain. Jackson observed patients suffering from epilepsy and other malfunctions of the brain most carefully, and correlated his observations with the condition of the brain as found in *post mortem* examinations. Guided only by the care of his observations, Jackson came to the conclusion that the sensory activity of the cortex is all confined to the rear of the central cross-fissure. Jackson also decided that the motor activity of the brain is all confined to the region of the cortex in front of the central cross-fissure. The suggestion of such localisation was revolutionary at the time, despite earlier work. However, Jackson's theory was quickly confirmed by Fritsch and Hitzig. Working with the brains of dogs, Fritsch and Hitzig found that they could cause certain muscles of a dog to move by weak electrical stimulation of the region of the brain in front of the central cross-fissure. If the right-hand side of the brain was stimulated, then muscles on the left side of the animal moved, while stimulation of the left-hand side of the brain caused movement of

muscles on the right of the animal. The same sort of stimulus applied to the regions of the brain behind the central fissure caused no muscular movement whatsoever. By observing which muscles moved in response to stimulation of a particular region, it was possible to make a map of the cortex showing which areas controlled which particular muscles.

Following earlier work, Ferrier refined the techniques used and found that quite detailed mapping of the motor surface of the cortex was possible. It was found that these movements of muscles produced by stimulation of the cortex were not simple reflex movements. Indeed, it seems that simple reflex movements cannot be produced by electrical excitation of the cortex but only by excitation of the spinal cord. Excitation of the motor region of the cortex produces more complex movements, such as a clutching of the hand. If part of the motor cortex is removed surgically, there is partial but not complete paralysis of the corresponding part of the body. Simple movements can be made but complex movements are impossible. It sometimes seems as though some muscles are being excited and inhibited at the same time. Where a muscle can be caused to contract by electrical stimulation of the cortex, it is sometimes found that the muscle movements can follow the stimulation even when this is as rapidly repeated as 100 or 200 times each second.

With the successful localisation of the motor cortex by electrical means, the way was open for extensive work on mapping the regions of the brain by many workers. The visual cortex in the occipital region has been mentioned, and there are other areas of various sizes in the part of the cortex to the rear of the central cross-fissure, all of which are connected with the different types of sensory nerve endings in the body. As Sherrington suggested, the brain seems to have evolved around the olfactory area because of the advantages obtained if the animal could associate this particular distance-sensitive sense with the senses of sight, sound, etc. It is interesting to note that the olfactory, optic and auditory areas have afferent fibres bringing information into the brain but few, if any, efferent fibres taking information to the muscles. This implies that these particular nerves must operate in the brain purely by association with the motor regions which, of course, have efferent fibres, and they cannot control muscles via the cortex in any other way. In this connection, there are some regions of the cortex which cannot be identified as either sensory or motor areas, but they have fibres coming from the sensory areas and other fibres going to the motor areas. These regions which are neither sensory nor motor areas are called association areas, since they seem to exist for the purposes of association of impulses from the various other regions. The area of

either the sensory or the motor cortex devoted to a particular part of the body does not depend on the size of the part of the body represented, but rather on the relative importance of that particular part to survival of the whole body. Thus the areas of the cortex associated with the hands are much larger than the areas associated with the arms, presumably because precise detail control of the parts of the hands is so very important. There are extensive 'silent areas', neither sensory nor motor, in the so-called prefrontal lobes in front of the motor areas of the brain. These prefrontal lobes will be discussed later.

When an attempt is made to detect the electrical impulses arriving in the sensory region of the cortex, there is a difficulty. As mentioned earlier, the surface of the cerebrum is in a constant state of rhythmic electrical activity and the resulting signals can mask the impulses arriving along afferent nerve fibres. Although certain electrical activity of the brain had been noted in earlier years, it was Berger in 1928 who first noted the rhythmic nature of this electrical activity. Six years later, using rather more refined apparatus, Adrian and Mathews verified that the brain is in a state of ceaseless electrical oscillation.

Scientists who had previously been content to investigate the activity of single, isolated, nerve fibres were now able to observe the activity of cortical nerve cells in the mass. Special machines for recording the electrical activity were designed, and these 'electro-encephalographs' have been used widely. There are more than 50 such machines in use in this country, and this represents a considerable investment in capital and manpower. The main reason for this is that the recordings obtained from such a machine can indicate brain abnormalities and in some cases they can be used to predict latent abnormalities. A few machines are being used for other purposes; for example, one in Birmingham is being used for research in industrial psychology.

In order to use such a machine to record the electrical activity of a person's brain, a number of very light-weight electrodes, are attached to the person's scalp. The electrodes are connected to the recording machine which has several pens, one for each of the electrodes. Beneath the pens lies a strip of paper which can be drawn along under the pens by an electric motor.

If an electrical signal appears at any one of the electrodes, the corresponding pen moves as the electrical signal varies. As the paper strip is moved steadily under the pens, the pens draw lines and as the electrical signals vary so the lines move from side to side on the strip of paper. If the electrodes have been fitted to a person's scalp, rhythmic electrical signals are picked up through the thickness of the

skull bones. The pens in the recorder vibrate in sympathy with the rhythmic brain signals, and a trace is therefore drawn on the strip of paper. When Berger first discovered such rhythmic electrical activity in the brain, he noticed two different ranges of frequency of vibration. One, which he called the alpha rhythm, corresponds to somewhere between 8 and 13 vibrations per second. The second of Berger's frequency ranges, which he called the beta rhythm, corresponds to something between 18 and 30 vibrations per second. Since those early days other rhythms have been noted. The theta rhythm, anywhere between 4 and 7 vibrations per second, was noted by Walter in 1943. An earlier discovery was the very slow delta rhythm of between $\frac{1}{2}$ and $3\frac{1}{2}$ vibrations per second. Walter has stated that delta rhythm seems an appropriate name, since this particular form of activity is associated with disease, degeneration and death and with the defences of the body against disease.

4

Action and Silence

The electroencephalograph has been of outstanding use in diagnostic medicine for the detection of brain tumours and of latent epilepsy. Tumours can interfere with the pattern of cerebral electrical activity and this interference can be detected by an experienced investigator from the trace on the strip of paper. During an epileptic attack, the electrical activity of the brain becomes greatly magnified. The trace swings violently and large 'spikes' of activity appear. Such activity only occurs during an attack, the electroencephalogram appearing quite normal at other times. However, it is possible to produce a degree of abnormality in the brain rhythms of people liable to epilepsy by having them stare at a light which flickers on and off at an appropriate number of times each second. It seems that the flickering light can trigger off the epileptic brain abnormality. There have been a number of cases in which a person has attempted to adjust a faulty television receiver which had a badly flickering picture. In so doing, they have brought their face close to the flickering light of the television screen and the flicker has induced an epileptic attack.

A similar procedure has been used for diagnostic purposes in the detection of latent epilepsy in an apparently normal person. A bright, flashing light is placed before the eyes of the subject while his brain rhythms are being recorded on the electroencephalograph. If the light flashes an appropriate number of times per second, it is possible to cause corresponding violent rhythms to appear on the recording paper in a small percentage of cases. This is naturally true when latent epilepsy is present, but it is also encountered in the brains of a few apparently normal people. When the light shining on the eyes flashes repeatedly, strange moving patterns appear to float in front of the eyes and sometimes there is a feeling of faintness.

The descriptions of the sensations caused by the flickering light are very similar to the description of their symptoms given by some sufferers from migraine.

The normal alpha rhythm is not constant in form; the trace of the electroencephalogram changes with variations in the mental and physical states of the person being examined. When he first started to investigate the electrical activity of the brain, Berger noticed that the alpha rhythm was greatly reduced in amplitude if the subject opened his eyes and looked at something, or even if he tried to look at something in a darkened room. The amplitude of the alpha rhythm is also reduced if the subject concentrates hard on a problem such as a mental sum. The alpha rhythm is most commonly found to the rear of the brain in the parietal and occipital regions. Various theories have been advanced to try to explain the reason for the existence of the alpha rhythms. One of the most popular is that the alpha rhythm is the manifestation of a scanning mechanism which scans all of the sensory inputs of the brain. This theory is advanced partly because of the coincidence of reaction time, i.e. the time which the brain takes to react to a stimulus, and the time taken for each complete vibration of the alpha rhythm. In addition, there is the fact that the alpha rhythm virtually ceases when one's attention is fixed on something. However, this latter fact introduces a difficulty when one tries to envisage such a scanning mechanism. The difficulty lies in conceiving some mechanism which would restart a scanning mechanism once it had stopped and the attention was riveted to something of interest. The fact that one is pondering a problem does not always prevent one from taking evasive action if a car is about to run one down. This happens to absent-minded professors but not to the average person, who seems to continue scanning for fresh information even when concentrating. All other theories of the alpha rhythm appear to lead to similar difficulties. Is it possible that this electrical rhythm is simply caused by large numbers of nerve cells carrying out in unison a process known to electrical engineers as relaxation oscillation? We know that the cells in the layers of the cortex are roughly arranged in lines, with each line a hundred or so cells long. A linear assembly of cells like this might well carry out a relaxation oscillation. If they did, and if some of the cells were pre-excited by incoming fibres, the frequency of the relaxation oscillation would increase and its amplitude would decrease, just as happens to the alpha rhythm when the brain is active.

In order to produce relaxation oscillation, rather specific electrical characteristics would be required of the cells. It is coincidental that the correct sort of electrical characteristic occurs as an interface

effect in liquids containing a certain amount of dissolved oxygen. Two further coincidences are that brain activity is vitally dependent on the presence of the correct amount of oxygen dissolved in the haemoglobin of the blood, and the fact that the whole of the nervous activity of the body depends on interface effects. To a layman such coincidences are quite remarkable, and there is a great temptation to make wild guesses.

Let it be stated right away that the real nature of the Berger rhythms seems to be a mystery even to those closely connected with its investigation. It is therefore of interest to spend a little time considering just what is known about them. The first point of note is that the patterns produced on the paper strip are quite exclusive to the individual, like fingerprints. Even identical twins do not have identical electroencephalograms. Although the shapes of the wave patterns change in childhood, they vary remarkably little after the age of 14 or so has been passed. In the very small child the electrical activity of the brain consists mainly of low frequency delta rhythms—electrical vibrations occurring between 1 and 7 times every 2 seconds. As the child becomes older and more active, the rhythms speed up. The delta rhythm is present only when the older child is asleep, while when the child is awake the brain produces the higher frequency theta rhythms—between 4 and 7 electrical vibrations each second. From the age of 4 onwards the even higher frequencies of the alpha rhythm, 8 to 13 electrical vibrations each second, begin to appear in the brain. Theta rhythms can appear in the adult brain. When they do there seems to be some correlation between the presence of theta rhythms and a general feeling of annoyance or frustration. Such a statement is not very scientific, since we cannot measure 'feeling of annoyance'. However, it is certainly true that the interruption of a mildly pleasant stimulus can cause theta rhythms to build up slowly and then suddenly to be replaced by the normal alpha rhythms several seconds after cessation of the stimulus. A lamp flashing in front of the eyes at the frequency of the theta rhythms can cause an induced theta rhythm to appear in the brain, and the subject sometimes experiences a feeling of annoyance at the same time. Walter has pointed out that at least these are facts determined from repeatable experiments.

The slow delta rhythms of childhood appear in the brain of the healthy adult only when sleeping. As a person gradually drops off to sleep, the frequency of the Berger rhythms falls. The normal alpha rhythms give way first to theta rhythms as light sleep commences, and then to delta rhythms when sleep is really deep. It should be mentioned that sometimes it is reported that rhythms are completely absent in deep sleep, though it seems that slow rhythms do

appear as part of the process of going to sleep. It is just as though, if we think in terms of the relaxation oscillation postulated earlier, the frequency of oscillation falls as the inputs to various cells are inhibited from firing the cells. Such inhibition could in effect return the brain to that early childhood state in which one can guess that there were few formed interconnections between nerve cells. In a subject where even the experts can only guess, the layman is tempted to make his own hypotheses. The nature of sleep itself is a mystery to all; indeed, there does not seem to be any valid reason why sleep is necessary at all.

Is it possible that sleep is in fact the ultimate objective of a living creature? Sleep is not possible until all disturbing factors such as hunger, danger and so on have been removed or at least accepted. Is not the homeostasis of the living creature directed to this very end? When homeostasis has temporarily achieved its object, the creature sleeps until a fresh disturbance of hunger, danger, etc. indicates that the homeostatic process must start again (and, we can guess, incidentally breaks up the slow delta oscillation of sleep into the faster oscillation of wakefulness). In more advanced animals inhibition can alter the picture somewhat, and such animals can learn as they grow older that sleep should sometimes be postponed until a more opportune moment. We can but conjecture. The one known fact is that as sleep comes on the electrical rhythms of the brain slow down.

It is interesting to note that the alpha rhythm activity is not affected by hypnotism. A hypnotic trance is not a state of sleep. At the present time hypnotism is yet another unexplained scientific mystery. And yet the fact that such strange patterns and even hallucinations can be caused by a mere flashing light makes it less surprising that a hypnotic state can be produced by the actions of a dynamic personality. It is possible that investigations of the Berger rhythms might give a clue to the nature of hypnotism. For example, it has been noticed that if a hypnotised subject with eyes closed, and consequently with pronounced alpha rhythms, is told that his eyes are open, then he appears to believe that they actually are open. However, his alpha rhythm does not reduce in amplitude as it should if his eyes really were open. Clearly, the whole brain does not accept the hypnotic suggestion.

The importance of dissolved oxygen in the action of the brain has been mentioned above. Glucose is another important constituent, but it seems that oxygen is the really basic necessity. A brain short of oxygen is incapable of detecting the shortage and of taking corrective action. Excessive carbon dioxide can be detected by the brain and this fact can help to avoid suffocation. However, in carbon monoxide

poisoning, such as is caused by motor car exhaust fumes or by coal gas, there is no warning signal from the brain. The person suffering the poisoning simply faints when the oxygen content of the haemoglobin falls to about one-half of normal. Lack of oxygen in the haemoglobin in the brain can cause lasting brain damage if it persists for more than a few seconds. A percentage of children are born as spastics. Certain parts of their bodies cannot be controlled properly, the brain being incapable of imposing the necessary fine control of movement. The reason appears to be that in these unfortunate cases oxygen is slow to reach the brain cells when the child has just been born. The cells are starved of oxygen for a short time and permanent damage results.

Lorente de Nó has concluded from his experimental work on nerve conduction that the really essential factor in producing an electrical discharge across the sheath of a nerve fibre is available oxygen. It will be seen that dissolved oxygen is of basic importance in nervous activity. It is not clear why. In searching for reasons, scientists can but continue to make hypotheses and then to test them by experiment until, one day, a hypothesis is found which reveals the underlying simplicity hidden below the confusing mass of experimental data which has accumulated on the subject. Even this will not be the ultimate hypothesis. We can suspect from past history that each advance in knowledge will solve old mysteries but at the same time it will uncover new ones. There is no reason to suppose that this process will ever come to an end.

There have been attempts to assess personality on the basis of electroencephalograms. Some people have a very persistent alpha rhythm which will not disappear even when the person is thinking hard and has his eyes open. It has been suggested that such people tend not to think visually, while people who think almost entirely in terms of visual images, in general have little or no alpha rhythm present under any circumstances. Most people have alpha rhythms which vary as the eyes open and close and as the concentration on a problem varies. Care is necessary in drawing conclusions from these facts, however. It must be remembered that observing the alpha rhythm and drawing detailed conclusions from it might be compared with attempting to assess the public opinion of a large body of people by asking them all to shout out their opinions at once. If the majority of the people are singing a rhythmic song while the rest of them shout out their opinions, it would be an almost impossible task to assess the average public opinion by observing the quickening and slowing of the rhythm of the song. No doubt something could be deduced from the rhythm of the song, but it is by no means clear just what this something would be. As an analogy the above leaves much

to be desired, but the intention is to stress the fact that caution is desirable in the interpretation of Berger rhythms.

Berger rhythms are found mainly in the occipital and parietal regions at the rear of the brain. The extensive regions of the cortex in front of the motor regions, the frontal lobes, are rarely found to be producing rhythms. For this reason, the frontal lobes are occasionally referred to as the silent region of the brain, as mentioned earlier. Not only does there seem to be little rhythmic activity here, but electrical excitation of this part of the cortex produces no effect on the body. These extensive frontal regions also do not appear to be directly affected by stimulation of the sensory nerves. The strange thing is that it is these very silent areas which constitute the biggest difference between the brains of animals and that of man. As evolution has proceeded, the frontal regions of the brain have increased in size and the shape of the skull has changed to accommodate the increase. This evolution has continued even in man, for the skull of early man could not house the brain of a modern man.

A clue to the function of the frontal lobes of the brain came in the middle of the nineteenth century. A man named Phideas Gage, working in a quarry in the United States, had drilled a hole in some rock and was tamping home an explosive charge with a steel crowbar. Suddenly the charge exploded, firing the crowbar through the man's face and up through his skull, severely damaging the frontal lobes of his brain. The wound healed and despite the damage to his brain the man recovered sufficiently to return to work. Although the normal functions of the brain as a controller of the body were apparently unimpaired by the accident, the man's personality had changed completely. He became an utterly self-centred person who cared for no one but himself. From this it appeared that the frontal lobes of the brain had something to do with the control of personality.

Many scientists, Pavlov included, have experimented with the removal of parts of the cortex of animals in attempts to localise brain function, and such experiments continue today. In the 1930s it was found that removal of the frontal lobes of chimpanzees calmed them down and reduced their normal excitability when frustrated. This process was applied to human beings by Moniz in an attempt to cure acute anxiety states. Moniz was successful, and since his time this operation of pre-frontal lobotomy or leucotomy has been performed on thousands of mental patients all over the world. The operation is a comparatively simple one to perform. A thin-bladed knife is introduced into the brain, often through a hole made in the skull at the front of the temple, just behind the eye. The knife is then moved around in order to cut the connecting fibres between the frontal

lobes and the rest of the brain. To a layman it sounds like rather a haphazard operation, and certainly an engineer would hesitate to draw concrete conclusions from the results of such an uncontrolled procedure. However, it does seem that in many cases the operation has succeeded in reducing or in removing the anxiety state which was previously a severe handicap to the patient. There seems to be a measure of success in about 60 per cent of the operations. There are often personality changes, however, and these can take the form of increased selfishness. The intelligence quotient or IQ is sometimes not reduced by the operation. There are various psychological tests, including those involving the assembly together of objects, which leucotomised patients sometimes cannot perform.

Similar personality changes can be produced in a like haphazard manner, but with less permanent injury, by passing electric currents through the brain. This is the well-known 'shock treatment'. Some further clue to the function of these silent areas can be obtained by considering differences between the behaviour of animals at various levels of evolution. Such an investigation is almost equivalent to asking the question, 'What basic features of the behaviour of the higher animals actually make it obvious that the animals are indeed higher?' As we have seen earlier, very simple forms of life are almost entirely reflex in action. They behave as they do because they are built that way. Reflex behaviour is infallible, an organism repeating a reflex action in response to a given stimulus even to the point of exhaustion. Slightly higher forms of life have patterns of behaviour which are not completely automatic and infallible. These are the -tropisms and the -taxis which have been mentioned earlier. They are intended to assist the homeostasis of the organism, but because of their very complexity they cannot be infallible.

Early on the evolutionary scale, the possibility of conditioning begins to appear. Remember that the whole object of the behaviour of any organism appears to be survival of the organism and of the species. Conditioning of reflexes helps this survival by providing anticipation and prediction of the future environment. Reflex inhibition is apparently a feature of the internal systems of animals, and as one proceeds along the evolutionary scale conditioning of inhibition as well as conditioning of reflexes begins to appear. This provision for the possibility of reflex inhibition is important to survival. It helps to prevent the 'fools rush in' type of action. In still higher animals, the complexity of conditioned action increases as does the complexity of conditioned inhibition.

It seems that as the frontal lobes of the brain increase in size, so does the capacity for inhibition of reflex activity. Although there is no certainty, such a correlation is probably more than coincidence.

As J. Z. Young has pointed out, great development of the extreme front part of the brain is characteristic of the higher apes and of man, and it seems that its influence is largely one of inhibition. There is a good case for defining intelligence in terms of inhibition (indeed, Thurstone did just this as early as 1924).* Planning and thought are involved in putting off actions until an opportune moment, and we can guess that this planning and thought are controlled by the frontal lobes of the brain.

When the frontal lobes are removed or damaged, as in leucotomy, inhibition is reduced and the leucotomised person tends to carry out only conditioned reflex actions. Such a statement is rather too precise for such an uncontrolled operation as leucotomy, and one expects, and frequently finds, a great variability in the results of such an operation. The complexity of conditioned reflex action is still marvellous and it is still directed to homeostasis and survival. It is the higher refinements of inhibition which are drastically reduced. This is not to say that all inhibition is localised in the frontal lobes. Indeed, Pavlov was led to suspect from the results of his experiments on dogs involving the removal of other parts of the cortex, that this tended to reduce inhibition and that conditioned reflexes could be established more strongly than before. Nevertheless, the great influence of the frontal lobes on the process of inhibition gradually becomes more apparent.

One of the characteristics which separates man from the other animals is his capacity for speech. The primitive cries given by lower animals are probably purely reflex, though because of their relative complexity perhaps it is better to term them instinctive. There are suspicions that these cries can be conditioned, but communication between the more primitive animals is on a very low level. It is possible with patience to teach a chimpanzee to say a few human words. There must be some sort of communication between those animals which form herds, and even between insects. However, it is only in man that the full power of communication by vocalisation has developed. It is probably no exaggeration to ascribe the growth of human civilisation largely to man's faculty for communication. The conditioned-reflex cries of the lower animals are uttered in response to the state of the external world. However, in addition, apes make sounds which are conditioned to thought. A less pompous way of expressing the same thing is to state that apes inhibit their natural cries until a more opportune moment presents itself. Such an inhibition of action is found even more strongly in humans.

Like other animals, early man formed herds, which we usually

*The writer wishes to thank the Editor of the Series for pointing out Thurstone's anticipation of this concept.

call tribes. Unlike other animals, as man evolved he found that he could pass on to others in his tribe any information which he had found useful to survival. There are attempts to do this at a much lower level. For example, von Frisch has shown how bees perform a complex dance which is believed to indicate the location of food to other bees from the same hive. However, man alone had the facility for communicating quite complex ideas, and he alone had the type of brain which could control the muscles to produce coherent speech. When he did communicate ideas to others he found that it would often aid his own survival, and this encouraged the further development of the means of communication. It is interesting to note that there are no sensory nerves sending signals back to the brain from the muscles of the tongue, only efferent muscles from the brain to the tongue muscles. The only feedback to the brain in this case is via other sensory fibres, including those in the ear. The nerve fibres from the ear, like those from the nose and eyes, are afferent to the brain only. These incoming fibres can therefore only be of use if they can be associated with one another and with the motor activity of other nerves, including those efferent fibres to the tongue. The brain provides a site for such association.

The characteristic of man is not simply that he is a tool-using creature. Monkeys are capable of enough inhibition to use a stick in order to extend their reach and so to obtain otherwise inaccessible food. The characteristic of man is that, having done such a thing, he communicates the information to other men. In his early tribes man found how to make axes and how to use them. He inhibited his natural fear of fire and learned how to preserve and to make fire for his own use. He learned how to do such things and he realised that it would do him no harm, and it might do him some good, to tell other men how to do such things. The mutual interchange of information over the ages led to the invention of spears and then to bows and arrows. Man acquired some sense of the passage of time and somehow he learned to plant seeds. Once he had learned this and had communicated the information to others in his tribe, he no longer needed to live as a nomad, for ever wandering in search of food. He could settle near his crops and shelter in a cave from the weather. Eventually, the interchange of information and the mutual co-operation made it possible for man to construct crude shelters and houses, villages, farms and towns. By communicating his ideas to others, man had made civilisation possible. This process took many, many thousands of years, but it was inexorable once man had found how to communicate complex ideas to his fellows.

The original object of man's civilising process is quite clear. It was to improve the chances of survival of the individual and of the

tribe. If anyone hindered the process and threatened survival, then let him beware! The thin coating of apparent altruism could easily be thrown aside. Inhibition need not be exerted when survival is directly in peril, and fierce defensive reflexes can then come into play. The weapons intended for use against animals could equally well be used against men. Intelligent man could even make use of his inhibition to prepare well in advance for battle and to plan the best tactics. And sometimes the best defence is attack. Thus did man attain his state of semi-civilisation based on wars and defence. The man of today differs little from his distant ancestors, for a few thousands of years are nothing on the time scale of evolution. Still man communicates to man the means of destruction.

5

Patterns

In order to be able to communicate his ideas, man had to be capable of remembering them himself. The simplest form of memory is the conditioned reflex which is found even in the lower animals. Evolution has made possible the elaboration of conditioning to the point where quite complex concepts can be remembered. The exact physical process by which concepts are remembered is still rather a mystery. There seems to be a certain amount of storage by recirculation, nerve impulses circulating around a closed path of fibres in the central nervous system. However, while this means of storage of associations could well provide for a short-term memory, it is unlikely that permanent memories are stored in this way. If they were, even momentary interruption of the recirculation of impulses would cause all past memories to be lost irrevocably. Instead, it is found, for example in cases of severe concussion, that the memory is lost for a short time only and then returns gradually. It therefore seems likely that long-term memories are based on some permanent change in the nerve pathways, possibly on some chemical change produced by the recirculating short-term memories. J. Z. Young has investigated the regeneration of damaged nerve fibres in an attempt to discover something about the process by which the body changes its nervous pathways. Nerve fibres which are not used tend to atrophy or to change in form and lose all possibility of functioning correctly. Like any other part of the body, a nerve fibre which is frequently used tends to grow and develop. A nerve fibre which is not used might disappear completely. However, when an attempt is made to apply this knowledge to deduce the functioning of the brain, the sheer complexity of the task makes progress difficult. One puzzling fact about permanent memory is that quite extensive parts of the brain can be removed or damaged without affecting memory at all. It is therefore probable that stored memories are not localised but are spread out in the cortex. Recent investigations

of this, as described by Sperry, have involved the isolation of parts of the brain with strips of electrical insulating material, as well as their removal.

An engineer attempting to design a memory device to remember as does the brain would find it hopelessly inefficient to attempt to store every sensory impression individually. It is much more efficient only to attempt to store associations between sensory impulses, and to reinforce those stored associations which are frequently repeated. Looking at microphotographs of cross-sections of the cortex, showing cell nuclei forming long lines down through the layers, the engineer is likely to think that here is a method of association of nervous impulses which is simple and which would work successfully. Those lines of cells in which many cells are excited can conduct more strongly, or perhaps at a higher rhythmic frequency, than can those lines of cells in which but few cells are excited. The outgoing fibres (axons) from the inner end of the cortex would then tend to grow if they came from lines of cells which were stimulated in association often, while the axons would tend to atrophy if they came from lines of cells which were rarely associated. Unfortunately, the fact that enormous numbers of cells would be required in such an associating mechanism tends to dissuade the engineer from attempting to build such a device and to persuade him to seek for simpler brain analogues.

Whatever the actual mechanism by which the brain and the body store memories, it is clear that the process is largely one of storing patterns. In all that the animal does there is a conscious or unconscious attempt to detect an underlying pattern, a number of basic features common to a number of different external situations. The recognition of such patterns greatly simplifies the task of memory. In effect, instead of an attempt to remember all of the details of a situation, the situation is associated with other situations having the same general pattern of events. The importance of pattern recognition can be seen all through human affairs. In reading, we recognise the shape of a word and associate it with a meaning. When we recognise someone who we know, we recognise the pattern of their face. In listening to a tune, we recognise the pattern formed by the notes. This latter case is most interesting because it illustrates a basic fact about pattern recognition. A tune can be recognised regardless of the key in which it is played. A tune played in a different key is not regarded as a different tune. Similarly a letter such as A can be recognised even if it is tilted or on its side.

One has to learn to recognise shapes, this is not an instinctive function. We know this mainly from the reactions of people who, though born blind, have been given sight by medical intervention

when they have already matured. The first thing which someone who has gained sight in this way does when he opens his eyes for the first time is to close them again quickly. The novel disruption of the normal patterns of activity of his nervous system is painful. When at last the new experience can be tolerated, only a distorted and moving coloured pattern can be perceived. The effect must be rather like that of migraine. It takes a long time before shapes can be appreciated, and it takes many months of training before the brain is able to associate the visual impressions with other impressions and so give them meaning. The differences between squares, triangles and circles are not obvious, they must be learnt laboriously. It must be rather frustrating, like trying to waggle the ears. Eventually, one learns to interpret the information coming in from the retina and the sight is normal. Even if only one eye is used to see with, the shapes which can be appreciated visually can vary in two dimensions in space and also in time. On the other hand a single ear can only appreciate patterns varying in one dimension (frequency) and in time, and it is therefore more likely to be profitable to think about the simpler auditory pattern-recognition system than about the visual system.

If one listens to the music of a jazz musician such as Louis Armstrong, one finds that he can 'mess around' with a tune to such an extent that the notes being played appear not to bear any direct relationship to the basic melody, and yet the performance is still recognisable as being based on a particular tune. In actual fact, the performance is not based on a melody, a sequence of notes, but rather it is based on a sequence of chords. Provided that the note being played at any instant bears a relationship to the chord sequence, then the performance does not sound wrong. This following of the chord sequence is a basic process in all improvisation and in much written music. It is possible for a number of musicians to play together, all simultaneously improvising around a given chord sequence. This collective improvisation can perhaps best be heard in the recordings made in the 1920's by the King Oliver band. The fact that it is possible to recognise music by chord sequence indicates that it is the chord pattern which is important rather than the individual notes. The notes themselves are important because many tunes can follow the same chord sequence, but it is really the relationship between successive notes which must be remembered. The brain must be capable of carrying out comparisons of pitch between successive notes if tunes are to be recognised.

If this mode of thought is extended, it will be seen that the brain must have some means of comparison of stimuli in order to recognise shapes and patterns. For example, to detect the difference between

a square and a rectangle visually it is necessary to compare the length of one side with another. The brain can certainly do this, though it is not yet known how the comparison is carried out.

Present-day civilisation is based on man's appreciation of pattern and on his communication of patterns to other men. Knowingly or unknowingly, the human race has for thousands of years been attempting to recognise the underlying patterns in the bewildering array of natural phenomena. Much of science is man's search for basic patterns which will simplify his concepts of the universe. Often the pattern adopted is too complicated, as witness the ages of discussion over the paths of the planets. Often it is too simple, as witness early views on atomic structure. Nevertheless, such patterns help science to decide on methods of investigation which will inevitably render the old patterns unsatisfactory and suggest newer and more satisfactory patterns which, at the same time, explain a wider range of natural phenomena. As in science, so in mathematics. The mathematician uses symbols to convey concepts where words take up too much room or are inadequate to the task. He learns the rules of manipulating these symbols and then he manipulates his symbols until he has made them produce a recognisable pattern, similar to one which he has seen before. In this way he discovers relationships between his symbols. In some cases the pattern of symbols suggests a pattern which is familiar in the real universe, and the mathematics can be applied to science.

Our present state of semi-civilisation seems to have been produced largely by communication of patterns between men. These patterns are what we usually call 'ideas'. It is necessary for us to ask 'What was the original advantage of pattern recognition which caused it to be favoured by natural selection?' A possible answer is that pattern recognition enables an animal to operate with a limited amount of information and also to predict the future course of events in the external world. These two features of animal activity are made possible by the recognition of a pattern which is only partially complete and the appreciation of what is required in order to complete the pattern. Recognition of a partially completed pattern is most important. For example, a number or a letter which is only partly drawn can be recognised despite the missing part. In fact, so well is this process carried out that sometimes the fact that a letter lacks one stroke is not even noticed.

The value of the recognition of incomplete patterns in the struggle for survival is clear. If an animal always had to wait until the whole of a situation was recognised in all its detail before it could proceed with an action, then it might postpone its action for too long and perish as a result. The fact that an animal can appreciate just

what is required in order to complete an external pattern implies that it is capable of predicting the completion of the pattern if previously learned associations give it a guide. In some cases such a procedure enables the animal to take evasive action and so improve its chances of survival. In other cases such a procedure enables the animal to lie in wait for food and so increase its chances of survival.

Pattern recognition calls for a complex form of conditioning of reflexes involving the association of the stimulation of many sensory nerves. Pattern recognition can also involve conditioning of inhibition. In some cases it is advantageous to hold off an action until a pattern of stimulation is complete or almost complete. It is often necessary to try to fit a pattern of events into a similar remembered pattern before a decision can be made on whether or not to proceed with an action. Such an attempt is made by finding some small part of the external pattern which is familiar, and then attempting to extend the correspondence between the external pattern and some pattern stored in the memory. This complex process is in effect one of the various activities which we call 'thinking'.

It has been suggested by Hebb that pain is experienced when a well-known stable pattern is disrupted. Some forms of pain are excited by special pain-producing nerve fibres which appear in reflex arcs intended to cause the body to remove the source of pain in the interests of survival. These pain reflexes can be conditioned like many other reflexes and the pain signals can be associated with other signals so that the organism can learn to avoid pain whenever it is threatened. Unlike other nerve fibres, the pain nerve fibres should not be carrying signals as part of the everyday activity of the body. The occurrence of signals in these pain fibres should be an unusual event. Consequently there should be none of the usual trivial associations which are certain to be found with other types of nerve ending. It is the patterns produced by the signals, often trivial, from the other nerve fibres which are the normal nervous patterns to which the body is accustomed. Signals coming along pain fibres are unusual. They can be expected to disrupt the normal pattern of nervous activity. The body then takes action in an attempt to remove the pain and to restore a more normal pattern. One of the actions is likely to be a good loud yell, relic of a primeval attempt to frighten away the cause of the pain or perhaps to attract help. Hunger produces very similar effects to pain. Indeed, it has been suggested that to a small baby they are identical. Certainly the small child reacts in the same way to either hunger or pain. It is possible to condition the body to accept pain and to ignore it. However, if this is done there is a risk that since the body is no longer being warned of danger, serious damage can occur.

It has been suggested that the infant must learn how to distinguish pain from hunger and to associate pain with various movements, environments and happenings. It is also possible that the reactions corresponding to pleasure must be learned. If pain disrupts the patterns of life, then does pleasure complete them? Perhaps the entire object of the actions of an organism is to complete that pattern which Nature, in the form of instinct, says is the correct pattern for survival.

Let us carry out an exercise in pure speculation. It has been stated earlier that the rhythms of the brain slow down in sleep to a state reminiscent of childhood. Could this slow rhythm be the basic rhythm of brain activity? When information is coming along nerve fibres to the brain it can cause the slow rhythm to be broken up. The brain tries to weave this extraneous interference into a dream, to examine the stored associations and then, if there appears to be no danger, sleep can continue. Eventually more and more signals, for example of hunger, will disrupt the slow oscillation and the frequency of the rhythm will increase. When a sufficient number of inputs appears, inhibition of outgoing impulses from the brain is removed and wakefulness returns. Through the waking hours attempts are made to satisfy the body's needs for survival and to remove those nagging inputs preventing sleep. In the higher animals, some of the reflex ways of removing these inputs will be inhibited for a longer or shorter time, planning ahead, accepting a reduced state now in the expectation of an improved state later, waiting perhaps years for the appearance of the right combination of conditions for action. The object is not only survival now but also survival at a later date. However, on this particular day it is possible to remove most of the disturbing inputs. The frequency of the Berger rhythm falls again and sleep returns.

The small baby sleeps much of the time (if its mother is lucky), but as it grows older it is necessary for the child to remain awake for longer and longer periods in order to survive. It becomes a habit, not too difficult to break, to sleep at night rather than in the daytime. Perhaps the nature of sleep holds the clue to the principles of operation of the brain. No doubt future research will solve the mystery. In the meantime, we know that fatigue does occur in nerves and it is just possible that sleep enables the nervous system to recuperate, but one would expect a few minutes of relaxation would be enough for this. It is of interest in this connection to consider that extreme form of sleep—hibernation. Those animals which hibernate do so when the body temperature falls. At low temperatures the activity of the nervous system is reduced. The metabolism of the animal changes so that it can survive with a

lowered body temperature and with reduced nervous activity. The process seems to be controlled from deeper centres in the brain, but the cortex is quite incapable of electrical activity at reduced temperatures. Hibernation at least seems to have little to do with recuperation and it appears more likely that it is a way of putting the animal in cold storage for the winter, when normal activity is difficult or impossible.

When a human sleeps, some of the action of the body is very much like a modified and reduced form of hibernation. The heart beats more slowly, the blood pressure falls, the metabolism is low. It is interesting to note, as have Best and Taylor, that one tends to be sleepy after a meal when an increased amount of blood must flow to the stomach to assist digestion, so consequently less blood can flow to the brain. The similarity between our sleep and true hibernation is striking, especially when one notes that extreme cold causes a human to sleep even though this is the wrong thing to do if the human is to survive. In order to sleep it is necessary to reduce the stimulation of the sensory nerves to a minimum. A comfortable and warm surface is required by the skin, in order to reduce the signals from the touch and heat nerves. The eyes are closed so that there is no stimulation of the retinal nerves. The muscles are relaxed so that the impulses coming from the muscles via sensory fibres are reduced. It does seem that when a sufficient number of disturbing inputs to the brain have been removed, sleep results and it continues until fresh disturbances, internal or external, end it. Sleep can be inhibited, particularly by the higher animals, if this is likely to be to the ultimate advantage of the animal in the battle for survival. Some people, admittedly rare, manage without sleep at all. Others find that after a few days and nights without sleep they suffer from hallucinations and illusions. Sleep remains a mystery and we can only guess at its real function. There have been enormous advances recently in the scientific study of sleep, particularly by Kleitman. In guessing, the danger of over-simplification must be avoided, but so must the danger of over-complication. The layman has the advantage over the professional in speculation because he does not have to use his speculation to suggest tests which might verify or destroy the speculation. As has been seen in the foregoing discussion of nervous activity, there is much which is still speculative. Today the engineer, speculating as a layman on physiology, can try out some of his ideas on machines which he can build. Even physiologists find such work interesting and sometimes it is also useful. Let us, then, now look at some of the work which has been done on the design and construction of machines which simulate the actions and controls of the animal body.

6

Cybernetics

In the Dark Ages men discovered how to make simple mechanical clocks which would record the time rather better than the sundials, sand-glasses, candles and water-clocks which had been used earlier.* By the seventeenth century, the simple clock had been elaborated by the addition of all sorts of mechanical devices. There seemed to be no end to the cleverness of the clockmakers. They appeared to be able to duplicate anything which moved. The aristocracy of the time were delighted with such toys and, tiring of simple fountains in the gardens of their palaces, they encouraged their hydraulic engineers to build hydraulically operated garden toys similar to those made by the clockmakers.

As we have seen, it was in such an atmosphere that Descartes began to ponder about the human body. He had been much impressed by Harvey's discovery of the circulation of the blood, and he compared this with the miracles of hydraulic engineering in aristocratic gardens. He also compared the veins with the tubular nerves and came to the conclusion that a hydraulically operated animal could be built, indistinguishable from a real animal. In those days Galileo had just been persecuted for his science and it was necessary for Descartes to take care. In addition, it is likely that he had deeply religious views. Although he moved house some twenty-four times in only a few years, in each case he made sure that his new house was very near to a cathedral as well as to a university. Whatever the reason, Descartes insisted that there was a fundamental difference between man and the animals in that an animal has no soul. He even postulated a site in the human brain at which soul and brain met. In his *Discourse on Method* he stated

*These and other aspects of the problem of measuring and estimating time are discussed in another volume in this series, *Time, Experience and Behaviour* by J. E. Orme.

clearly, 'It is morally impossible that there should be sufficient diversity in any machine to allow it to act in all the events of life in the same way as our reason causes us to act.' Many would still agree with his opinion today.

We must acknowledge Descartes as the father of what is now called cybernetics. Those who followed him were even more mystical and little more was done in the comparison of animals with machines for a few hundred years. With the coming of the Industrial Revolution, as Wiener has pointed out, men became vitally interested in the concept of a machine as an efficient piece of energy-conversion equipment. It is only in the twentieth century that inefficient machines capable of processing information rather than power have become important. The trend began with early attempts to replace the old visual methods of telecommunication, such as beacons, smoke signals and the semaphore, by electrical methods. Telegraph engineers and, later, telephone engineers used metal wires to carry information long distances from one point to another. Maxwell investigated the theory of wave motion, and he suggested not only that light is radiated in the form of electromagnetic waves, but that similar, though non-visible, radiation at lower frequencies should be possible. Over the next years, many people carried out experimental investigations intended to test the theories of Maxwell. In Germany, Hertz attempted to detect magnetic effects in non-conductors of electricity by passing high-frequency electric currents through large pieces of paraffin wax. To his surprise, he found that the magnetic effects could be detected a considerable distance from the paraffin wax, and that the effects were still there even if the wax was removed from the electrical circuit. Thus the effect did not depend on the wax at all. Almost by accident, Hertz had verified Maxwell's predictions. Indeed, years earlier in London, Hughes had demonstrated this effect, but unfortunately a number of the most eminent scientists of the day had discouraged him from further work by claiming that it was all well known. Commercial exploitation of the work of the physicists spread rapidly as the new wireless telegraph, based on the work of Maxwell and Hertz, was applied, and improved methods were invented. Men were now for the first time actively interested in inefficient machines, in electrical devices in which the output power was a tiny fraction of the power supplied. It did not matter that huge quantities of power were expended if this led to the transference of important information from one place to another.

Radio was greatly improved when electronic valves were invented. The transmission and reception of speech became simplified. From the tiny electrical signals received by an elevated antenna,

the valves could amplify them until the signals became of sufficient power to operate even a loudspeaker. Gradually, it was realised that the electronic valve was a power amplifier which took the tiny power of the received signals and used this to control much larger powers coming from the receiver supply battery or electric mains supply. From the time that they were invented, valves were also used in telegraphy and telephony to increase the power levels of the weak received signals.

Valve amplifiers, stationed at intervals along a long telephone line, made possible telephone communication at enormous distances. Telephone engineers wanted to improve their amplifiers. In radio it was not unusual to take some of the output signal and return it to the input, adding it to the input signal. This form of feedback, often called reaction or regeneration, increased the amplification of an amplifier. However, it also reduced the quality of the amplification, the faithfulness with which the output signal followed the input signal. It could also cause the amplifier to give a continuous howl of oscillation if there was too much signal feedback.

If this additive, positive feedback caused a degradation of the quality of amplification and a danger of oscillation, was it possible that subtractive, negative feedback could improve the quality and remove the danger of oscillation? This negative feedback could be obtained by taking some of the output signal and returning it to the input but subtracting it from the input signal. Negative feedback was tried and it was found that the quality of amplification could be improved. However, it was also found that there was still a danger of oscillation. Under some circumstances negative feedback could actually become positive feedback and oscillation could result. Once further work had revealed the reason for the spurious oscillation, it was possible to avoid the danger by using special techniques when designing an amplifier incorporating such negative feedback.

Negative feedback was not a new thing. It had been used on machines for years. When Watt wanted to maintain constant the speed of his steam engines despite variations of load, the steam engine governor was invented. In this, the engine caused two weights to rotate at the ends of two levers. As the engine speeded up it rotated the weights at the ends of their levers like the chairs on the ends of their chains on a chairoplane roundabout. The faster the engine rotated, the further did the weights swing out, moving their supporting levers as they did so. The levers were used to move the throttle of the steam engine, admitting less steam as the weights flew outwards and so tending to reduce the speed of the engine. In this way, if for any reason the speed of the engine increased, then the governor weights flew outwards and restored the speed to its

correct value. The governor acts by negative feedback in that it controls the steam supply in such a way as to oppose the variation of speed. If the operator wanted to vary the speed deliberately, he had only to adjust the governor movement. Only a small power was required in order to carry out the adjustment and this small power could control the very much larger power produced by the steam engine. In this way power amplification was incorporated in addition to negative feedback.

In the terminology of today, the steam engine governor is called a regulator. Many forms of regulator have been used, and for many other purposes than the control of steam-engine speed. The basic features of a regulator are a measuring and comparing device and a power amplifier. For example, voltage regulators are often fitted to electrical generators. The output voltage of the generator is compared with a fixed voltage. The difference between the two voltages is used to control the generator so that if for any reason the generator voltage tends to rise above the correct value, the regulator prevents the rise from being more than a very small amount. As with the feedback amplifier, it is possible for the negative feedback to become falsely positive in certain circumstances and it is necessary to design the regulator carefully to avoid this, since otherwise oscillation might result. The resultant violent swinging up and down of the generator output voltage would be most undesirable.

When a heavy weight had to be moved, at one time it was necessary to assemble a number of men or animals to use their combined strength. This is still true in many parts of the world, but in more advanced places machinery can be used. The essential feature of such a machine is power amplification, the control of a large amount of power by a small amount of power. A single man exerting only a small effort and therefore using little power can control a very large machine capable of moving an extremely heavy weight. One type of machine includes a device which produces an electrical voltage dependent in value on the position of the heavy weight. This voltage can be compared with another voltage set by the operator. The difference between the two voltages can then be used as the input to a power amplifier which controls the large machine. Such an arrangement is called a servo-system, after the Latin word meaning 'slave'. The basic characteristics of a servo-system are power amplification, measurement and comparison as for a regulator, but the term 'servo' is usually reserved for devices which control mechanical movement. The operation of all of these closed-loop systems is based on negative feedback, and once again the negative feedback can become positive and oscillation can result if precautions are not taken at the design stage. Oscillation

in a large servo-system would be very undesirable, since heavy weights would be moving to and fro in an uncontrolled manner.

When war came in 1939, servo-systems were being used in military as well as in civil control equipment. Servos were used to control large guns and searchlights in response to low power signals, at first from hand cranks or levers moved by a human operator and later from electrical signals coming from a radar set. During the war many scientists investigated the properties of feedback systems and this sort of work has continued ever since. Today attempts are being made to construct adaptive servo-systems. These are servo-systems in which the power amplifiers are self-adjusting in order to obtain the best overall servo characteristics and to avoid oscillation.

At the same time as the effects of negative feedback were being investigated in the 1930's, physiologists were beginning to think in terms of negative feedback when studying the animal nervous system. As we have seen, at first they did not use the term negative feedback at all, but Cannon introduced the concept of homeostasis in the autonomic nervous system. The nervous system acts as part of a regulator which maintains, for example, constant body temperature. In order to extend the concept of homeostasis to matters external to the body, the nervous system can be considered as part of the control apparatus by which the body differentiates itself from its surroundings and by which it carries out its entropy-reducing process. In its internal and external reactions, the body of a man or an animal acts as though it was a number of fairly complex regulator and servo-systems. These systems do not act independently, their activities are co-ordinated by the central nervous system. The aim is homeostasis and survival, both of the individual and of the species despite short and long-term environment changes.

In the mid-1940's, the common ground between engineers and physiologists began to be appreciated. Wiener, a mathematician, coined the name 'cybernetics' and he published a book[1] with this title in 1948. Although whole chapters of the book are mainly mathematical and bear little direct relationship to the control of organisms, the theme of the book is the extensive parallels between the operation of animal nervous systems and the feedback control systems of machines. Many scientific workers in various fields began to describe themselves, or to be described, as cyberneticians. The fact that Wiener included in his book much that can today be called information theory has unfortunately widened the field of cybernetics considerably. In the present context, we are interested in drawing parallels between organisms and machines and in methods of designing machines which have some of the attributes of organisms, and we shall not be dealing

directly with information theory and statistics. Let us then proceed with a critical review of work on such machines.

There have been various attempts to construct machines which, in their behaviour, show similarities to living organisms. Pask[2] has stated that he knew of over 350 machines of this type which have been either simulated by computer programmes or constructed as special mechanisms. The interest in this field has been growing at a fantastic rate in recent years. Simmons and Simmons[3] reviewed the literature in 1961 and they gave a curve showing the rapidly increasing rate at which information is being published in this field. In such a situation, no review can pretend to cover every item of work which has been reported, but it is possible to take an overall view of the progress which has been made by selecting items which are typical. The subject can be divided up into a number of overlapping segments:

simple machines
game-playing machines
special-purpose machines
artificial nerve cells
nerve cell assemblies
visual pattern recognition
speech recognition

Although the overlap between these segments is considerable and not everyone would use the same sub-divisions, they will be used here as a basis for a consideration of the 'state-of-the-art' of cybernetics.

McNaughton[4] has suggested that from the point of view of technology there is no valid reason for building another human being artificially, since we already have them in plentiful supply. This would seem to be a very narrow point of view, if meant seriously, since although the supply of the real thing is plentiful, the mechanism is but vaguely understood. From this viewpoint alone such work is justified. Where analysis is difficult, synthesis can often suggest a way of progress. In any case, we must assume that the advancement of human knowledge in any direction needs no justification from technology.

Ever since the time of Descartes there have been attempts to construct fairly simple automata. Some of these have been sheer trickery, as for example the Maelzel Chess Automaton, produced by von Kempelen in the late eighteenth century.[5] This was in fact controlled by a concealed dwarf human operator. It is said that on one occasion this became only too apparent when some joker yelled 'Fire!'

In recent years there have been more genuine attempts to con-

struct devices which can display some of the more advanced characteristics of living creatures. Although much of this work is supposed to be taken seriously, some of it must be regarded merely as the construction of new forms of scientific toy. These have often been given extravagant and pompous pseudo-scientific names. The serious object of the construction of such toys is the observation of behaviour in the hope that it will stimulate further and fruitful thought about the method of operation of animal and human nervous systems. The danger is that such toys can stimulate thought to the point where it becomes sheer fancy. Thus one experimenter in discussing the action of a very simple toy states that such models show inexplicable mood changes. This seems a rather unscientific way of thinking about a machine which comprises one microphone, one photo-electric cell and a few electronic valves and electric motors. One would hesitate to use the word 'mood' in discussing the behaviour of an earthworm, even in non-technical writing, although the mechanism of the earthworm is much more complicated and wonderful than is that of the toy in question.

While it is necessary to accept a great deal of flexibility of language when working in a new field, there are limits beyond which even the over-enthusiastic scientist should not be prepared to go. Flowery language leads to obscurity. The problem is that when working on something which is measurable a scientist is able to arrive at a terminology which has a defined and agreed meaning, while when trying to describe something which he does not yet know how to measure he has to fall back on the use of analogies. His work can then be made to appear to have an exaggerated importance to himself and to others if the analogies are well chosen.

REFERENCES

1. WIENER, N., *Cybernetics*, Wiley (1948)
2. PASK, G., 'A Discussion of Artificial Intelligence and Self-Organisation', *Advances in Computers*, **5**, 109 (1964)
3. SIMMONS, P. L., and SIMMONS, R. F., 'The Simulation of Cognitive Processes; An Annotated Bibliography', *Trans. I.R.E.*, **EC10**, 462 (1961); 535 (1962)
4. MCNAUGHTON, R., 'The Theory of Automata, A Survey', *Advances in Computers*, **2**, 379 (1961)
5. DUDLEY, H., and TARNOCZY, T. H., 'The Speaking Machine of Wolfgang von Kempelen', *J.A.S.A.*, **22**, 151 (1950)

7

Toys and Machines

Having warned ourselves of the danger of reading more than is justified into the action of a machine, let us consider some of the models which have been made. There have been many attempts to produce machines which could find their way through a maze by trial and error, and could then store the correct information about directions so that there was no need for future trial and error. Thus Ross built a machine which operated on a maze of model railway tracks. In 1952, Wallace[1] described a similar machine controlled by an electronic computer, while Ducrocq built a machine which displayed tropistic behaviour based on electric charges. Shannon[2] built a machine which could go through a maze without being restricted to tracks. Instead, an electrical contact finger could be moved in north–south or east–west directions through the maze by two different electric motors. The maze was a five-by-five array of 25 squares, some of which were partially surrounded by walls. Whenever the contact finger touched a wall, it was returned to the centre of the corresponding square to start again. The strategy used for searching through the maze depended in part on the previous experience of the machine. If the maze was not solved in a given number of moves, the memory was erased on the assumption that the machine was simply repeating a cycle of operations over and over again.

The fact that many insects behave very much like machines in the way that they follow instinctive tropisms has attracted workers to construct machines having built-in effects similar to tropisms. Thus Wiener, Wiesner and Singleton produced a simple tropistic machine. Berkeley[3] describes an artificial squirrel 'Squee' which searches for tennis balls, which it returns to its 'nest' for storage.

Walter[4] has produced several simple machines and the descriptions of some of these have been widely published. Thus 'Nerissa' was a Nerve Excitation, Inhibition and Synaptic Analogue,

while 'Cora' was a Conditioned Reflex Analogue. Walter also produced the well-known electro-mechanical robot 'Elmer', built in the form of a tortoise which wandered around the floor, being built on a steerable tricycle undercarriage. One form, which Walter refers to as 'Machina Speculatrix', contains two electronic valves, two relays and two motors. One motor drives the propulsion wheels of the device while the other can cause the steering wheels to change direction continuously. A photo-electric cell is mounted on the spindle of the steering wheels so that it scans around continuously as the steering wheels change direction. The electrical circuit is arranged to have the following action in response to the signals from the photocell:

	Drive motor	*Steering motor*
In the dark	Half-speed	Full speed
In moderate light	Full speed	Off
In strong light	Full speed	Half-speed

In addition to the photocell, this device has a 'shell' which closes an electrical contact whenever the device encounters a mechanical obstacle in its path. This contact is arranged to cause continuous oscillation between the 'dark' and the 'strong light' states whenever the shell touches an obstacle, one-third of the time then being spent in the 'dark' drive condition and two-thirds of the time in the 'strong light' drive condition. If the photocell is illuminated at the time of encountering an obstacle, the oscillation between states is speeded up, though the circuit is less sensitive to light while the device is touching an obstacle.

As seen from the above table, if a moderate light shines on to the photocell it stops rotating and remains directed at the light. Since the steering-wheels are coupled to the photocell, the drive motor then drives the machine in the direction of the light. However, if the light is too strong, the scanning does not cease. Walter refers to this as 'negative tropism to very bright lights'. Speed reduction is obtained by connecting a lamp in the circuit so as to divert some of the power from the drive motor. If the light from this lamp falls on the photocell, it too can affect the action and so complicate it further. Similarly, a mechanical obstacle repels the device, though this can be done equally well with a mechanical 'slipping drive' arrangement alone, as seen in some forms of children's 'flying saucer' mechanical toy. Walter elaborates extensively on the similarities which he can imagine between the action of this simple machine and that of living creatures.

Walter's conditioned reflex analogue is primarily a static device. Two switches provide the input stimuli, and coincidences between the two inputs are added together until a level is obtained at which a

slowly decaying oscillation can be initiated by the sum. This oscillation provides the slowly decaying memory of the coincidences. While this memory persists, the recurrence of one of the inputs on its own can cause an electrical relay to operate. Walter says that this device could be added to the mobile model described above, to elaborate its actions.

Angyan[5] produced a more elaborate version of Walter's mobile machine by adding sound-selective filters to the input and also an additional memory circuit. Both memories used thermistors (that is, resistors the values of which change with temperature) to replace the oscillating form of memory used by Walter. Angyan's machine, which he called 'Machina Reproducatrix', could respond to signals from a lamp, a flute or a whistle, and it could associate these signals in various ways. Angyan also provided built-in inhibitory circuits. Later Angyan, with Zemanek and Kretz,[6] considering the earlier machine to be inadequate, added a 'sleep' state to the machine, which they now called 'Machina Combinatrix'. This can assume 40 basic states. The writer's students have built a similar machine as shown in Fig. 3.

Fig. 3(a). Simple mobile associating machine

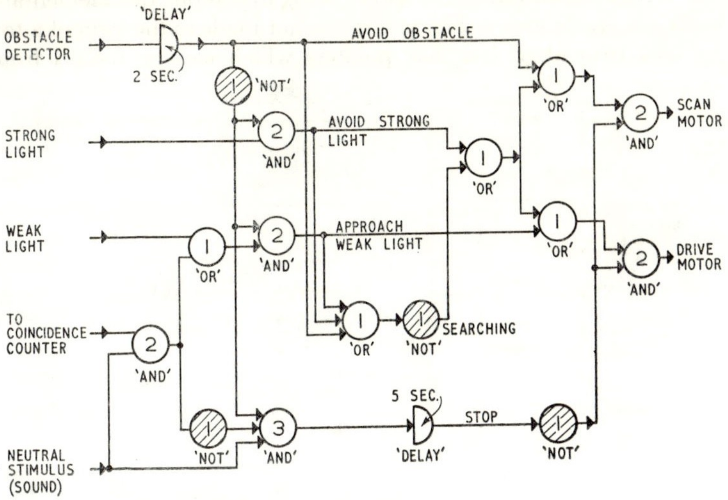

Fig. 3(b). Block diagram of the simple mobile associating machine

Andreae[7] introduced a mobile machine, 'Stella', which starts action with no prior information at all about its environment. Its movement is obstructed by illuminated walls which can be detected by the eight photocells on the machine. It has both short-term and long-term memory arrangements, the actions of which are based to some extent on the procedures used by Steinbuch[8] for his Learning Matrix.

The long-term memory includes a slow die-away to simulate forgetting. Andreae gives a block diagram and a flow diagram of his system. Based on this work, Andreae and Gains have considered the requirements for a learning machine to steer a car along a winding road. This work illustrates well the contrast in this field between the abstruse and often esoteric pseudo-mathematical analysis and the practical results obtained.

Huggins[9] built a simple mechanical toy dog to illustrate Pavlovian conditioning. The dog has a photocell concealed in its jaw, so that it can 'see' food. It also contains a microphone so that it can 'hear' a bell. 'Salivation' is indicated by the lighting-up of the dog's eyes. Despite the simplicity of the electrical circuits, conditioning can be demonstrated. It was also arranged that the dog would gradually 'forget' the association as time passed, and that repeated ringing of the bell in the absence of the reinforcement of food would cause a more rapid decay of the memory.

Ashby[10, 11] produced a widely-known simple machine which he

called the Homeostat, the intention being to demonstrate elementary homeostasis. As seen in Fig. 4, this was not made in the form of a toy animal. Instead, it has four pointers which can be moved from

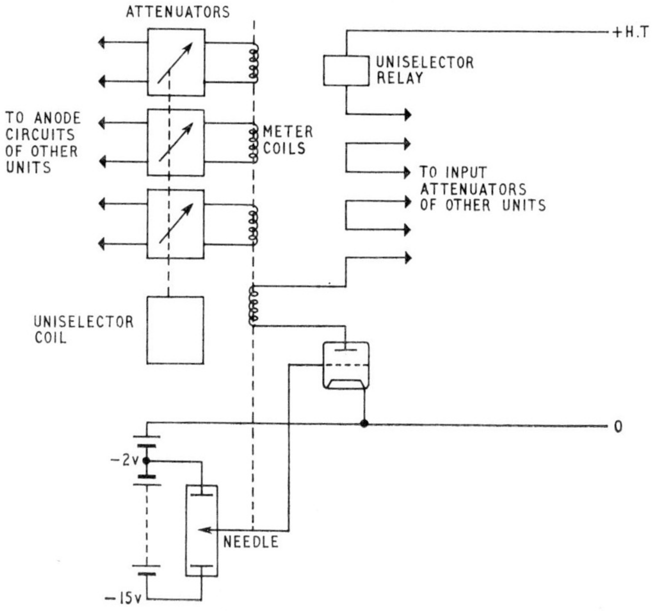

Fig. 4. Ashby's homeostat

side to side electrically. If any one of the pointers is moved from a central position, the electrical circuits are changed in a series of random steps until all four pointers are again moved to stable central positions. In effect, this Homeostat automatically follows a slow, and often prolonged, random trial and error procedure until it achieves a steady set of predetermined stable conditions whenever these conditions are disturbed. Ashby feels that this action is comparable with the process of homeostasis in animals. He has elaborated the simple principles on which this mechanism was based, in order to produce what he has called a design for a brain. The title of his book is perhaps a misnomer. After 238 pages the main conclusion obtained appears to be that evolution can make organisms homeostatic. Ashby has also produced other cybernetic machines, and he mentions that Kletsky has produced a static version of the homeostat, i.e. a version without the moving needles.

Ashby mentions that, unlike the usual forms of control system, if some of the connections are disturbed mechanically or electrically,

the homeostat can still achieve stability. This feature he calls ultrastability. However, it is sheer chance whether or when this condition will be achieved, since the search is simply made at random. The point has often been made that even a monkey, simply hitting typewriter keys at random, would eventually probably write all the plays of Shakespeare, provided that he was given enough centuries in which to continue his random activity.* Ashby seems to have mechanised this sort of action, but with much greater restriction of possible action, so that a recognisably stable set of conditions is achieved in a reasonable time. The homeostat cannot be said to have any purposeful aim. In effect, it just flounders about aimlessly, but if it happens by chance to find a comfortable position it stays there. Given the same initial conditions, it will repeat the process without learning.

MacKay[12] comments on this point, elementary but crucial, that Ashby's homeostat merely operates at random, with no information about the required direction of action. Consequently any particular action can possibly make matters worse than they were before. The action is not 'goal-guided'. MacKay distinguishes between 'goal-oriented' action, where only one action is possible, and 'goal-guided' action, where a choice between actions must be made. An example of goal-oriented action is that of a steel ball rolling after a magnet. On the other hand, the action of a thermostat in maintaining a constant temperature is goal-guided. MacKay also considers the possibility of introducing 'inventive' features into machine activity. MacKay's own simple machine[13] has a number of hoppers from which balls are dropped by the action of an electronic circuit. Each ball, as it drops, can affect the action of the electronic circuit which controls its own hopper. The electronic circuits are interconnected in such a way that, when a ball has dropped from a hopper, the probability of another ball dropping from the same hopper is reduced for a time. However, it is possible to insert in the path of one of the dropping balls an obstacle which has the effect that whenever a ball drops it increases (rather than decreases) the probability of another ball dropping from the same hopper. Eventually in this case balls fall from one hopper only. MacKay uses this simple machine to illustrate the reinforcing or the increase of the probability of successful actions from a random set.

Murray[14] proposed a simple machine using amplifiers operating electromechanical latching relays. This machine could modify its own circuitry and was intended as a verification of his theoretical

*In *Gulliver's Travels,* Swift describes a similar but slightly more efficient method of writing learned treatises, used by the Professor of Speculative Learning of the Academy of Lagado.

work on 'robots'. Wilkins[15] proposed a machine which he called 'Emma' (Eye Movement Memory Apparatus). By moving a mirror, a mosaic of photocells is enabled to scan a field of view at random. If an object comes into the field of view, the random search is suppressed and the object is 'fixated'. The memory built into the machine is then scanned to see if this is a new or a known object. Ingenious methods of determining the number of objects in a field of view have been proposed (see von Foerster[16]).

Uttley[17] has discussed the structure of the nervous system and has produced a number of machines based on what he calls 'conditional probability'. This is basically the notion of conditioned reflex associations as applied to simple machines. He draws parallels between the actions of his conditional probability system and the actions of various forms of positive and negative conditioning and inhibition in animals. He suggests that the practical problems involved in constructing such a machine are eased by the introduction of a continuous recovery (forgetting) process. Uttley shows that, when time is taken into account, two separate impulses of equal strengths appearing on two different nerve inputs can produce 12 different basic patterns. The actual pattern produced depends on the order of occurrence of the two inputs in time. Ingeniously, he uses musical notation to illustrate this fact, and he describes a simple machine capable of detecting such patterns. Uttley points out that it is necessary to introduce mechanisms to produce delayed versions of the nerve signals in order to detect such temporal patterns of activity. It is interesting to note that Scott and Williams[18] show that the information carried by a number of different nerve fibres at the same time will arrive in the form of a particular wave pattern if the fibres do not have identical speeds of conduction. The shape of the wave pattern in time will depend on which of the fibres are actually stimulated. In this way a 'spatial' pattern can be converted by simple nerve fibres into a 'temporal' pattern. Allanson[19] dismisses the inverse operation.

Later, Uttley[20] extended his earlier work. He pointed out that neurons at a higher level in a nervous system are inevitably fired less frequently than are those at the lower levels from which the inputs to the higher levels are derived. Details are given[21] of a machine using a hydraulic form of computer to count coincidences and thus indicate the probabilities of joint occurrence of two separate inputs. The circuits of an electronic version are also described.

Andrew[22] considered the possible application of the conditional probability type of machine to the control of industrial processes. He suggests that a logical-type learning machine with only 30 yes–no inputs would have to learn how to behave on the occurrence of

every one of the 2^{30} (or approximately 1,000 million) different combinations of inputs which might arrive, and this would inevitably take a long time. However, Andrew does not mention that such 'complete know-all' activity is not a characteristic of living creatures at all, and that it is in fact the characteristic which humans have often ascribed to their gods. He shows how impractical such a scheme would be if the memory were based on magnetic tape recording.

To come down to earth, the difficulty suggested by Andrew is somewhat artificial. Considering only 3 yes–no inputs, he provides memory for all of the 8 possible permutations of the inputs. However, if we consider the associations of the inputs in pairs, there are only three possibilities to be considered. With a number n of input channels, Andrew feels that 2^n storage locations are required in the memory. To consider the full implications of this, if there are 30 inputs and two of them happen always to occur in association inevitably, regardless of the condition of the other 28, Andrew would nevertheless use up 266 million separate storage locations to record this simple fact in the memory. Yet this fact is typical of the type which appears to be important to living organisms. It is clear that living organisms have a more economical system than that proposed by Andrew.

Based on his earlier ideas, Andrew[23] programmed a digital computer to simulate a simple optimising control system which maintains constant the liquid level in a tube despite random variations in the parameters of the system. Later, he programmed a digital computer for polynomial curve-fitting.[24]

Andrew[25] and Uttley[20] give photographs of the application of a simple conditional probability computer to the control of a small trolley. The trolley is intended to traverse the boundary between black- and white-painted regions on a board. It carries a lamp which illuminates the board, and two photo-electric cells which can be used to differentiate between light and dark areas on the board. The trolley moves forward provided that one photocell is over black and the other is over white. However, if both photocells are over a single colour, then the trolley searches from right to left until it locates a position where the photocells are straddling the boundary.

The left–right, black–white information is supplied to a conditional probability computer which learns the best direction in which to turn if both cells are over black or if both are over white. If the trolley is turned completely round, the stored information is now incorrect, but the computer gradually re-learns until the steering control is correct and the trolley moves forward while straddling black and white areas. This is quite an impressive performance for a

computer containing only about 30 units. Andrew[22] describes the principle of operation. The units are essentially occurrence counters which sum up the occurrences of individual inputs and of coincidences of inputs in pairs, threes, fours and fives. The counts are stored in the form of voltages on leaky electrical capacitors, so that 'forgetting' is built-in and more recent coincidences are more important than earlier ones. When any groups of inputs occur simultaneously, the machine computes the probability that other inputs are also present or are about to appear, based on the information stored on its capacitors.

Barlow[26] and Donaldson describe a possible machine for recording information to reduce redundancy. The operation is based on the measurement and comparison of probabilities. The incorporation of a decaying memory was suggested.

Gamba[27] discusses the theory of PAPA (Probabilistic Automatic Programmer-Analyser). It is based on the earlier work of Gamba,[28] in which the principle was proposed that inductive intelligence can be reduced solely to a calculus of probability. George[29] gives a general review of the machines of Uttley and of Pask, and he gives a photograph of his own simple machine. He also discusses the programming of a digital computer to learn, and continues his discussion later at greater length, though still generally.

REFERENCES

1. WALLACE, R. A., 'The Maze-Solving Computer', *Proc.A.C.M.*, 119 (1952)
2. SHANNON, C. E., 'Presentation of a Maze-Solving Machine', *Trans. 8th Conf. Josiah Macy Found.* (Ed. V. Foerster), 173 (1951)
3. BERKELEY, E. C., *Symbolic Logic and Intelligent Machines*, Chapman and Hall, 177 (1959)
4. WALTER, W. G., *The Living Brain*, Duckworth (1953)
5. ANGYAN, A. J., 'Machina Reproducatrix', *Mechanisation of Thought Processes*, **2**, 933, H.M.S.O. (1959)
6. ZEMANEK, H., KRETZ, H., and ANGYAN, A. J., 'A Model for Neurophysiological Functions', *Information Theory, 1960* (Ed. C. Cherry), 270, Butterworths (1961)
7. ANDREAE, J. H., 'Stella; A Scheme for a Learning Machine', *Automatic and Remote Control*, 497, Butterworths (1964)
8. STEINBUCH, K., 'Die Lernmatrix', *Kybernetik*, **1**, 36 (1961)
9. HUGGINS, P., 'Two Experimental Learning Machines', *J.I.E.E.*, **6**, 702 (1960)
10. ASHBY, W. R., 'Design for a Brain', *Electron. Engnrg.*, **20**, 379 (1948)
11. ASHBY, W. R., *Design for a Brain*, Chapman and Hall (1952)
12. MACKAY, D. M., 'Towards an Information-Flow Model of Human Behaviour', *Brit.J.Psych.*, **47**, 30 (1956)
13. MACKAY, D. M., 'The Epistomological Problem for Automata', *Automata Studies* (Ed. C. E. Shannon), 235, Princeton (1956)
14. MURRAY, F. J., 'Mechanisms and Robots', *J.A.C.M.*, **2**, 61 (1955)
15. WILKINS, B. R., 'Memory and Learning Circuits', *Industr. Electron.*, **1**, 96, 154 (1962)

16. VON FOERSTER, H., 'Biological Ideas for the Engineer', *New Scientist*, **15**, 305 (1962)
17. UTTLEY, A. M., 'The Classification of Signals in the Nervous System', *E.E.G. Clin. Neurophysiol.*, **6**, 479 (1954)
18. SCOTT, P., and WILLIAMS, K. G., 'A Note on Temporal Coding', *Inf. and Control*, **2**, 380 (1959)
19. ALLANSON, J. T., 'Some Properties of a Randomly Connected Neural Network', *Information Theory* (Ed. C. Cherry), 303, Butterworths (1956)
20. UTTLEY, A. M., 'Conditional Probability Computing', *Mechanisation of Thought Process*, **I**, H.M.S.O. (1959)
21. UTTLEY, A. M., 'The Design of Conditional Probability Computers', *Inf. and Control*, **2**, 1 (1959)
22. ANDREW, A. M., 'Learning Machines', *Mechanisation of Thought Processes*, **I**, 473; **II**, 945, H.M.S.O. (1959)
23. ANDREW, A. M., 'Self-Optimising Control Mechanism', *Automatic and Remote Control* (Ed. J. F. Coales), 636, Butterworths (1961)
24. ANDREW, A. M., 'An Experimental Comparison of Some Algorithms for Self-Organising Systems', *Trans. I.R.E.*, **IT8**, S163 (1962)
25. ANDREW, A. M., 'Machines Which Learn', *New Scientist*, **4**, 1388 (1958)
26. BARLOW, H. B., 'Sensory Mechanisms', *Mechanisation of Thought Processes*, **II**, 535, H.M.S.O. (1959)
27. GAMBA, A., 'Remarks on the Theory of PAPA', *Supp. Nuovo Cimento*, **26**, 169 (1962)
28. GAMBA, A., 'Optimum Performance of Learning Machines', *Proc.I.R.E.*, **49**, 348 (1961)
29. GEORGE, F. H., 'Cybernetic Models and their Applications', *Process Contr. Automat.*, **6**, 92; 422; 478 (1959)

8

Logic and Games

Mathematicians became attracted to the study of cybernetics quite naturally, and indeed Wiener himself was a mathematician. They have worked mainly in two fields, logical theory and game-playing machines. The former, including the so-called finite automata theory, does not appear to have led to concrete practical results. However, the latter has proved to be a means by which mathematical machine designers and computer programmers could astonish the general public with the tricks performed by their computers.

Such machines, capable of playing various games, have received much attention, partly on the grounds that here is a human activity amenable to at least partial mathematical analysis. For example, a number of workers have tackled the extremely complex problem of chess-playing machines. Byard[1] has reviewed various early game-playing machines and automata. Early in the present century, Queredo built a successful mechanical arrangement which could play against a human a simplified game of chess, using only three chessmen and only requiring one of five basic moves by the machine.

Before considering more recent attempts, it is as well to heed the warnings of Ashby[2] and Bellman[3] that, being artificial, the game of chess is unlike most natural situations with which humans have to deal. The problems dealt with by a chess-playing machine are not truly representative of a class of problems which a real mechanical brain will one day have to tackle.

Shannon[4, 13] wanted to programme a computer to play a skilful game, perhaps comparable to that of a good human player. He regarded this task as a preliminary to programming a computer to carry out such functions as the design of electronic circuits, language translation, orchestration of a melody, etc. He felt that the nature of the game of chess makes it a suitable subject for study, and it has

the advantage of being a game which is generally considered to require 'thinking'. However, Shannon points out that even with a fast computer as much as 16 minutes could be required for it to decide on each move, and that such a machine would not learn from its mistakes.

Shannon considered possible procedures without presenting an actual chess-playing programme. It is necessary for the machine to look forward at least a few moves and to consider the possible eventual effect of any particular move. The alternative of referring at each move to stored details of all possible positions and suggested moves is not practicable. Shannon also considered simple methods of altering the 'style' of playing.

Turing[5] analysed his own thought processes when playing chess and he suggested a computer programme based on these. He worked on the assumption that anything which could be explained in mathematical symbols and English could be used to form a computer programme. Samuel[6] described Turing's programme as a 'weak player'. Turing felt, however, that it should be possible to programme a computer to improve its game as it gained experience. Prinz[7] programmed a computer to solve 'mate-in-two' problems in chess, subject to certain restrictions.

Turing also considered the games of draughts and nim. A machine for playing the latter game was exhibited at the 1951 Festival of Britain, and it is described by Stuart-Williams[8]. In this game, objects are arranged in a number of unequal rows. For example, four rows are used, each containing up to seven objects. Each player in turn must take one or more objects from any one row. Each player attempts to force his opponent to take the last object. However, the game of nim is essentially trivial, since a procedure or algorism exists which will always ensure a win if followed.

Kister *et al.*[9] programmed a very much reduced game of chess, played on a 6 x 6 (rather than an 8 x 8) board, on to a digital computer and they demonstrated that the computer could beat a weak human player. The bishops were omitted and only six pawns were used on each side, while there was some restriction on the possible allowed moves. Investigating four moves ahead, 12 minutes were required to compute each move. Bernstein *et al.*[10, 11] produced another non-learning programme for chess playing which provides a passable amateurish game during opening and middle, but a weak finish to the game. Although the machine always responds in the same way to a given position without learning, the possible moves are very numerous and a human opponent is unable to predict them.

This programme takes about 8 minutes to compute each move

by 'looking ahead' four moves. At each move it analyses the possible consequences only of the seven most plausible moves. This involves examination of the 2,401 possible positions four moves ahead. These positions are analysed by answering eight questions similar to those which a human chess player asks himself.

Newell *et al.*[12] set out to use the game of chess to investigate human modes of thought. They wanted their machine not only to make good moves, but also to make them for the 'right' reasons. Consequently, they made a deliberate attempt to simulate human thought processes, even though this leads to great complication in the programming of the computer.

Bellman[3] regards chess as an inherently unstable game in that small differences in the positions of pieces and pawns can make all the difference between winning and losing, while the actual number of pieces and pawns on the board is often relatively unimportant.

Machine playing of a number of games other than chess has been investigated. Hagelbarger[14] built a machine to play a simple 'penny matching' game. It operates by extrapolating the past sequence of its opponent's moves into the future, and so it is called 'SEER' or Sequence Extrapolating Robot. It wins more games against human opponents than it loses, since the play of humans is not really random.

The machine is able to recognise and to take advantage of this fact. Several groups have used digital computers to simulate Hagelbarger's work. For example, Foulkes[15] describes a programme for determining the statistical structure of a sequence of 1's and 0's (e.g. 001001001001). The programme makes use of the statistical information discovered in order to predict the next symbol in a sequence. Similarly, Kochen and Galanter[16] describe the use of a computer to 'guess' the next event in a sequence which forms a definite pattern. Such work is, in effect, simulating the pattern-completion capabilities of living organisms.

Huggins[17] produced a machine to play a game using 17 counters. The machine and its human opponent remove one, two or three counters in turn, the object being to make one's opponent take the last counter. In order to guarantee a win with such a game, it is necessary not to make the first move and then always to make sure that the total number of counters removed by the two players adds up to four on each round. Huggins's machine plays at random at first, but it gradually improves its game by building up a record of the probabilities involved. Very little memory storage capacity is required in order to do this, and it is provided by rotary stepping switches. Huggins mentions that the introduction of a 'forgetting'

mechanism could further reduce the storage requirements. He suggests that one of the things shown by the machine is that order can be created out of the chaos of random numbers, though it is a slow process. This was in fact demonstrated by letting the machine play against random numbers obtained from dice. The correct winning moves are still gradually learned.

Martens[18] describes a programme which can enable a computer to learn to play simple board games such as noughts and crosses after 30 to 50 attempts, given no prior information except a rule for determining the 'legality' of moves. At the end of each game, the computer is informed whether the outcome was 'win', 'lose' or 'draw'. Martens also elaborates mathematically on the difficulty of defining what is meant by 'learning' behaviour.

Samuel[6, 19] describes a programme for teaching a machine to play a better game of checkers (draughts) than the programmer could play. This learning process takes 8 to 10 hours of machine playing time. The machine is given only the rules, a 'sense of direction' and some additional incomplete information about the game. In 1960 Samuel[6] reviewed the whole field of game-playing computers, and he mentions the early work of Strachey with the game of checkers. In Samuel's computer programme for checkers he uses 32 of the 36 binary digits contained in a standard computer 'word' to indicate the 32 squares of one colour actually used on the board in this game. He describes how to compute lists of available moves from these computer 'words'. There is provision for learning so that the machine can improve its game. In fact, the machine can be programmed to act as two separate players simultaneously, so that it 'plays against itself'. Samuel compares the two different learning routines which he used. One gives a poor opening, the other a poor middle game.

Samuel mentions 'Lex', a digital computer programme for the game of bridge, originated by Lefkovitz. This involved searching in a computer table of possible plays, taking up to 15 seconds for each search. Horman[20] discussed a programme for learning the solution to the 'Tower of Hanoi' puzzle, in which a number of differently sized discs are piled in a cone formation on a peg. All of the discs must be moved one at a time from one peg to one of another two in the smallest possible number of moves, while preserving the original stacking order of the discs. It has been proved mathematically that if there are n discs, then the smallest possible number of moves to achieve success is $2n-1$. Other forms of puzzle have also been considered, for example, Michie [21] dealt with the sliding-block type of puzzle.

The other field which has been explored by mathematicians is

that of the possible mechanisation of operations in logic. Indeed, this field has received extensive investigation from the designers of digital computers, which can be thought of as based entirely on the mechanisation of the form of symbolic logic introduced by Boole. However, we are not here concerned with the design of the universal form of digital computer, but rather with more specialised forms of computer involving logical operations.

As an example, McCallum and Smith[22] described simple computers for the solution of logical problems. A typical problem suitable for their first machine is as follows: 'It is known that salesmen always tell the truth and engineers always tell lies. B and E are salesmen. C states that D is an engineer. A declares that B affirms that C asserts that D says that E insists that F denies that G is a salesman. If A is an engineer, how many engineers are there?' This is no trick question. There are four possible solutions to the problem, and in each case the answer is 'three'. The simplest model of their logical computer finds solutions by searching through all possibilities until one is found which satisfies the initial specification of the problem. This process is much too slow for use with more than a few variables such as ABCDEFG.

In order to overcome this problem, McCallum and Smith proposed feeding back the outputs of the computer to the inputs in such a way that a change is made only in any of the variables which violate the required conditions. In this way a rapid convergence towards one of the answers to a logical problem is obtained, and this is advantageous if only one, any one, of the possible solutions is required. However, it introduces the possibility of repeated 'hunting' around a number of unsatisfactory conditions without ever encountering a suitable answer to the problem at all. This can be avoided by making equally likely all of the possible changes from any given condition, so introducing an element of probability into the operation of the device. McCallum and Smith note that the type of logical problem solved quickly by this form of computer tends to be precisely that which is solved quickly by a human brain. Strangely, their work seems to have been largely neglected, perhaps because they did not make any exaggerated claims or flights of fancy.

Newell and Simon[23] specified the theory of a machine for discovering proofs of theorems in symbolic logic. Later, with Shaw,[24] they investigated by hand-simulation a computer programme which they called the General Problem Solver or GPS, which was intended to be used also for proving algebraic and trigonometric identities, integration and differentiation. Reitman[25] extended their work and considered the use of the GPS in, for example, composing music.

He also considered the Soviet work of M. M. Bongard on programmes for machine solution of such problems as:

A	B	C
4	2	8
9	3	27
5	5	5
2	4	X

Answer: $C = \frac{A^2}{B}$, so $X = 1$.

Such problems are typical of human intelligence tests. Reitman compared this with the pattern recognition work of Selfridge[26] and Dineen[27]. He mentions Feigenbaum's EPAM (Elementary Perceiver and Memoriser) computer programme and other similar work.

Gorn[28] made the point that the old 'Ancient Mariner' human gives a lengthy biographical sketch in the course of conversation before arriving at any conclusion about anything. This could well occur in a machine which incorporated an attempt to record every item of its experience, no matter how trivial. Gorn suggests that the reinforcement only of appropriate responses removes this problem, though the resulting action is then less 'intelligent' and more like brute habit-forming or like simple conditioning. He terms the former 'explicit' and the latter 'implicit' learning.

In 1936, Turing[29] published a study of an abstract idea for a computing machine. The machine he considered consisted of a very long tape, divided into squares, together with means for writing and reading symbols, letters, numbers, etc. in the squares and means for erasing symbols from the squares. The machine was also considered capable of moving the tape to right or left. Many mathematicians have considered the theoretical possibilities of such machines. One section of the tape can contain symbols which convey instructions to the machine (i.e. the machine 'programme'). In this case the machine is usually called a Universal Turing Machine, and its action resembles that of a modern digital computer. The theory of such machines is often called Automaton Theory.

McNaughton[30] suggests that while automaton theory seeks to study the logical and algebraic aspects of certain devices, cybernetics is the study of the statistical aspects of the same devices. He surveys the whole field of the theory of automata, as do Burks and Wang[31]. McNaughton also gives a simple but convincing argument that the probability is zero that any machine can last for ever, regardless of how often and in what manner parts are replaced. It follows that no individual biological organism can live for ever. Perhaps Nature is not so stupid after all in minimising the use it makes of regeneration of parts of the body. The only assumptions made in the argument are the plausible ones that the organism never exceeds a

certain size and that each part has a certain rate of decay. He draws the additional interesting conclusion that if ever the human population in the universe stops expanding, then the human race cannot last for ever.

Lofgren[32] considers how the use of redundant parts (i.e. the incorporation of more than the absolute functional minimum number of parts) can increase the reliability and reduce operational errors in complex automata. Arbib[33] proved the theoretical equivalence of Turing tape machines to models consisting of assemblies of neurons which had been suggested by McCulloch and Pitts[34]. However, much of the published theory of automata has little to do directly with cybernetic models, and the name is therefore rather unfortunate.

Digital computers have been programmed to carry out various applications allied to logical operations. Oettinger[35, 36] described two forms of programme used with the EDSAC computer. In the first, the machine is thought of as a child who is given a shopping list and who must discover which shops stock the required articles. The names of shops and a list of the articles stocked at each are stored in the computer, which searches at random in its memory to find the location of any required article. Once found, the information is stored and it can be used to reduce the necessary searching time on the next occasion that the same article is required. Oettinger suggests the addition of forgetfulness to make the action more natural. This work illustrates admirably the uses and limitations of analogies when thinking about machine operation. Oettinger also programmed EDSAC to behave as a conditioned-reflex machine which can be trained by an operator to give certain responses to input stimuli. The operation of this programme was quite successful, and surprisingly it did not require the entire information storage facilities of EDSAC. However, Oettinger felt that once the programme had been demonstrated successfully, it was of little further interest. It was successfully shown that a standard digital computer can be used as a simple learning machine merely by adding a special input tape.

Farley and Clark[37], following Turing, say that provided the rules of organisation of a given system are known, then it can always be simulated as closely as desired by a digital computer, no matter how complex is the organisation of the system. They refer to learning with 'short-performance' inputs as 'conditioning', while learning with 'long-performance' inputs is called 'serial learning'. They feel that simulation with a digital computer is better than the construction of special analogue machines, since programming a computer is quicker than constructing a special analogue device. They felt that

their work successfully demonstrated the modification of activity with experience.

Friedberg[38] simulated both a learning machine and its teacher on a digital computer, which is arranged automatically to modify its own programme to achieve a desired result. Later the difficulty of deciding on the meaning of the results, considering the small size of the machine, was pointed out. Gelernter and Rochester[39] describe a programme which can produce proofs of theorems in elementary Euclidean plane geometry. Also Gelernter[40] further discussed procedures for producing geometry proofs on a digital computer. Holden and Johnson[41] describe the use of a digital computer to prove trigonometric identities. George[42, 43] gives a general discussion of programming a digital computer to learn.

REFERENCES

1. BYARD, S., 'Robots which Play Games', *Science News*, **16**, 65, Penguin (1950)
2. ASHBY, W. R., *An Introduction to Cybernetics*, Wiley (1956); (Chapman and Hall, 1956)
3. BELLMAN, R., 'Dynamic Programming, Intelligent Machines and Self-Organising Systems', *Proc. Symp. Math. Theory Automata*, Polytechnic, 1 (1963)
4. SHANNON, C. E., 'Programming a Computer for Playing Chess', *Phil. Mag.*, **41**, 256 (1950)
5. 'Digital Computers Applied to Games', *Faster than Thought* (Ed. B. V. Bowden), Ch. 25, 286, Pitman (1953)
6. SAMUEL, A. L., 'Programming Computers to Play Games', *Advances in Computers*, **1**, 165 (1960)
7. PRINZ, D. G., 'Robot Chess', *Research*, **5**, 261 (1952)
8. STUART-WILLIAMS, R., 'Nimrod', *Electron. Eng.*, **23**, 344 (1951)
9. KISTER, J., *et al.*, 'Experiments in Chess', *J.A.C.M.*, **4**, 174 (1957)
10. BERNSTEIN, A., and ROBERTS, M. DE V., 'Computer vs. Chess-Player', *Sci.Amer.*, **198**, 96 (1958)
11. BERNSTEIN, A., *et al.*, 'A Chess-Playing Program for the IBM 704', *W.J.C.C.*, **15**, 157 (1959)
12. NEWELL, A., SHAW, J. C., and SIMON, H. A., 'Chess-Playing Programmes and the Problem of Complexity', *I.B.M.J.*, **2**, 320 (1958)
13. SHANNON, C. E., 'A Chess-Playing Machine', *Sci.Amer.*, **182**, 48 (1950)
14. HAGELBARGER, D. W., 'SEER, A Sequence-Extrapolating Robot', *Trans.I.R.E.*, **EC5**, 1 (1956)
15. FOULKES, J. D., 'A Class of Machines Which Determine the Statistical Structure of a Sequence of Characters', *I.R.E., Wiscon.*, **3**, (4), 66 (1959)
16. KOCHEN, N., and GALANTER, E. H., 'The Acquisition and Utilisation of Information in Problem-Solving and Thinking', *Inf. and Control*, **1**, 267 (1958)
17. HUGGINS, P., 'Two Experimental Learning Machines', *J.I.E.E.*, **6**, 702 (1960)
18. MARTENS, H. H., 'Two Notes on Machine Learning', *Inf. and Control*, **2**, 364 (1959)
19. SAMUEL, A. L., 'Some Studies in Machine Learning Using the Game of Checkers', *I.B.M.J.*, **3**, 211 (1959)
20. HORMAN, A., 'Programs for Machine Learning, Pt. 2', *Inf. and Control*, **7**, 55 (1964)
21. MICHIE, D., 'Machine Intelligence', *Penguin Science Survey B*, 55, Penguin (1965)

22. MCCALLUM, D. M., and SMITH, J. B., '1. Mechanised Reasoning; 2. Feedback Logical Computers', *Electron. Eng.*, **23**, 126; 458 (1951)

23. NEWELL, A., AND SIMON, H. A., 'The Logic Theory Machine, A Complex Information-Processing System', *Trans.I.R.E.*, **IT2**, 61 (1956)

24. NEWELL, A., SHAW, J. C., and SIMON, H. A., 'A Variety of Intelligent Learning,' in *Self-Organising Systems* (Ed. M. C. Yovits and S. Cameron), 153, Pergamon (1960)

25. REITMAN, W. B., 'Programming Intelligent Problem Solvers', *Trans. I.R.E.* **HFE2**, 26 (1961)

26. SELFRIDGE, O. G., 'Pattern Recognition and Modern Computers', *Proc. W.J.C.C.*, **7**, 91 (1955)

27. DINEEN, G. P., 'Programming Pattern-Recognition', *Proc. W.J.C.C.*, **7**, 94 (1955)

28. GORN, S., 'On the Mechanical Simulation of Habit-Forming and Learning', *Inf. and Control*, **2**, 226 (1959)

29. TURING, A. M., 'On Computable Numbers with an Application to the Entscheidungsproblem', *Proc.Lond.Math.Soc.*, **2**, 42 (1937)

30. MCNAUGHTON, R., 'The Theory of Automata, A Survey', *Advances in Computers*, **2**, 379 (1961)

31. BURKS, A. W., and WANG, H., 'The Logic of Automata', *J.A.C.M.*, **4**, 193, 279 (1957)

32. LOFGREN, L., 'Automata of High Complexity and Methods of Increasing Their Reliability by Redundancy', *Inf. and Control*, **1**, 127 (1958)

33. ARBIB, M., 'Turing Machines, Finite Automata and Neural Nets', *J.A.C.M.*, **8**, 467 (1961)

34. MCCULLOCH, W. S., and PITTS, W. A., 'A Logical Calculus of the Ideas Immanent in Nervous Activity', *Bull. Math. Biophys.*, **5**, 115 (1943)

35. OETTINGER, A. G., 'Programming a Digital Computer to Learn', *Phil. Mag.*, **43**, 1243 (1952)

36. OETTINGER, A. G., 'Simple Learning by a Digital Computer', *Proc. A.C.M.*, **9**, 1 (1952)

37. FARLEY, B., and CLARK, W., 'Simulation of Self-Organising Systems by Digital Computer', *Trans. I.R.E.*, **IT4**, 76 (1954)

38. FRIEDBERG, R. M., 'A Learning Machine', *I.B.M.J.*, **2**, 2 (1958); **3**, 282 (1959)

39. GELERNTER, H. L., and ROCHESTER, N., 'Intelligent Behaviour in Problem Solving Machines., *I.B.M.J.*, **2**, 336 (1958)

40. GELERNTER, H., 'Machine-Generated Problem-Solving Graphs', *Proc. Symp. Math. Theory of Automata*, Polytechnic, 179 (1963)

41. HOLDEN, A. D., and JOHNSON, D. L., 'Simulation of Human Problem-Solving Methods', *Proc. N.E.C.*, **19**, 489 (1963)

42. GEORGE, F. H., 'Probabilistic Machines', *Automation Prog.*, **3**, 19 (1958)

43. GEORGE, F. H., 'Cybernetics and Inductive Programming', *Process Contr. Automat.*, **6**, 422; 478 (1959)

9

Special-Purpose Machines

A large part of the work on cybernetics which has been discussed so far has been concerned with toys and with games. Perhaps by now the reader is beginning to think that cybernetics is just another scientific recreation, and certainly much of the work discussed in the previous chapters can be put in that category. One really cannot blame scientists for making a hobby of their work if they can. Indeed, they always have and let us hope that they always will, for when scientific investigation becomes a mere duty then progress will rapidly stop. The scientist who is fascinated by the universe and its wonders is often the one who has sufficient interest to try to find out what 'makes it tick'.

However, to reassure the reader that cybernetics is not all hobby, let us now consider a few fields where the concepts have been found useful in aiding the progress of more workaday applications. Cybernetics includes both communication and control, and applications to both of these spheres of the techniques suggested by its study have been investigated.

The fact that Morse code appears to be formed from a succession of only two types of symbol, dots and dashes, has long made it seem suitable for decoding by automatic machines. For example Babcock[1] describes a Morse code translator in which 'weights' are allocated to each character depending on the number of dots and dashes it contains. A flash tube then illuminates the correct character on a rotating fluorescent disc so that it becomes visible for a time. Later, Hayton *et al.*[2] considered ways of automatic conversion from one type of telegraph code to another, while Carter and Wheeler[3] produced electronic methods of converting between Morse code and teleprinter signals. However, all of this early work relied on the very uniform characteristics of Morse code signals produced by a machine, and there was little serious attempt to decode automatically Morse signals produced by a human being.

In fact, there are more than two symbols used in Morse code,

since the lengths of the intervals between the dots and dashes also convey information. This would not cause insuperable problems in decoding and neither would variations of speed. However, when Morse signals are sent by a human operator by hand, the lengths in time of the symbols are very inconsistent, and each operator has his own individual style of sending, which can sometimes be recognised by another operator. Despite the idiosyncrasies of hand-sent Morse code, a human operator at the receiving end is quite capable of successful decoding, and it is therefore a challenge to attempt to devise a machine to do the same.

A certain amount of work in this direction has been reported in the United States. Gold[4] described a special-purpose, non-learning, digital computer known as 'MAUDE' (Morse Automatic Decoder). This achieved between 90 and 95% success in decoding the Morse code hand-sent by 184 different operators. Selfridge and Neisser[5] also discussed MAUDE, together with their own 'PANDEMONIUM' learning system for character recognition, which was described by Selfridge.[6] McElwain and Evens[7] discussed the correction (or 'degarbling') of the English text after decoding by MAUDE, on the assumption that some prior information is given about the permissible message-words. More recently, Shepard[8] has suggested that a human recognises Morse code mainly by the length and internal complexity (or heterogeneity) of the Morse symbols. For example, the Morse symbol for R (· — ·) is more heterogeneous than that for U (· · —), which is in turn more heterogeneous than the symbol for S (. . .).

The stenotype machine used by American court-room stenographers was developed by Ireland early in this century. It has 22 keys, each of which can print a phonetic symbol in a particular column on a 3 in.-wide paper tape. Any number of keys can be struck at the same time, so making possible a code consisting of a great many combinations of symbols. An extra key is used as a shift key for numerals. Speaking speeds as high as 175 words per minute can be written using this machine, but it can take as long as four hours to transcribe tape corresponding to only one hour of speech. An investigation has been made[9] into the possibility of programming a digital computer to carry out the transcription. This is not as easy as might be thought at first sight. For example, 'Over here' and 'Overhear' can only be distinguished by making use of the context.

In his book *Cybernetics*, Wiener mentioned the possible use of artificial limbs incorporating muscles controlled by signals derived from the human nervous system. There are two basic forms of muscle substitute. One form actuates prostheses, or replacements for amputated parts of the body, while the other form actuates

ortheses, or aids for paralysed limbs. By 1960, Kobrinski *et al.*[10] were able to describe an artificial hand controlled by electric nerve signals picked up from human muscles, for example, from the nerves in the stump of a partly amputated human arm. Separate signals are obtained from the muscles normally closing the hand and from those which normally open the hand. These signals are used to operate an electric motor moving the prosthesis in small steps, the direction of the steps depending on the picked-up muscle signals. Special devices are fitted to feed back to the operator signals indicating, for example, the pressure exerted by the artificial hand. Some of the feedback information used by the human for control was found to come from the sound and vibration of the electric motors operating the artificial hand. Tomovic[11] made an artificial hand in which physiological feedback signals come from the changes of electrical resistance of carbon-impregnated sponges contained within the 'skin' of the artificial hand.

Bottomley *et al.*[12] suggest that there is a widespread feeling that because electrical actuators are so heavy and noisy, pneumatically operated prostheses are to be preferred. These have the additional advantage that storage of the required operating energy in the form of compressed gas is easier and lighter in weight than the equivalent storage batteries required for electrically operated devices. They mention work which seems to indicate that it will be necessary to pick up and co-ordinate the signals from several muscles in order to obtain a more natural movement. Their own work is largely in the interpretation of the nerve signals and on methods of overcoming difficulties such as 'backlash'. Bottomley and Cowell[13] describe, with photograph, a two-hook artificial hand controlled from amplified nerve signals. An Italian artificial hand prosthesis was described by Horn.[14]

Basmajian[15] found that, if they are provided with feedback of an amplified nerve signal on a loudspeaker, some human subjects are able, with care and practice, to control a single nerve fibre at will. This can be done even though the resulting muscular movement is imperceptible in the absence of the amplification. Perhaps this is akin to the extreme acuity of vision which many people with defective vision acquire for a time when they are first fitted with spectacles. Harrison[16] described his own work in the field of prosthetics, in particular the control of an artificial leg-brace with signals obtained from nerve fibres.

Vodovnik and McLeod[17] describe a method of control of a muscle involving electronic by-passing of a broken nerve fibre, using signals picked up from a completely different muscle. For example, they proposed the control of the right forearm with signals

derived from muscles in the left shoulder. They mention the possible danger of electric shock, only too painfully encountered by others in this work. They minimise this danger by having the muscle-stimulating electrodes very close together.

A very interesting investigation into the control system of the pupil of the human eye was carried out by Stark.[18] He found that the response of the pupil to light variations decreases rapidly if the variations are more rapid than about three every two seconds. Thus although the pupil opens and closes in unison with low-speed light variations of intensity of illumination, it no longer has time to move fully as the rapidity of the variations is increased. The response falls off very steeply as the frequency of variation of light intensity is increased, and the theory of servo-mechanisms predicts that sustained oscillation should be possible in such a case. However, the gain (i.e. the sensitivity of the pupil to changes of light intensity) is so small that this oscillation does not occur. Stark artificially increased the effective sensitivity of the pupil-size control mechanism by shining a small bright spot of light on to the edge only of the pupil. He found that the predicted continuous oscillation of pupil size could indeed be produced. Medically, this would be called an 'induced pupillary hippus'.

Using this experimental method, Stark was able to produce a simple mathematical expression for the response of the human pupil control system to changes of light. His expression included a pure latent time delay of 0.18 sec, which is surprisingly long considering that nerve impulses would probably take less than 0.02 sec to travel from retina to cortex and back to the muscle. Katznelson and Gould[19] also considered the theory of the eye-pupil control system. Induced hippus was first observed by Stern,[20] later work being reported by Campbell and Whiteside[21] in 1950 and by Stark *et al.*[22-24] in 1957 and 1958.

The way in which the animal nervous control system can adapt to changes in itself and in its environment has attracted the attention of the designers of servo control systems. Such a capability would be very desirable in some servo-systems. As a simple example, consider the auto-pilot of an aeroplane, which should preferably be capable of controlling the aircraft at all points in its flight. Unfortunately, the control characteristics of an aircraft are not constant during the flight. For example, there are changes of weight as the fuel is used up, and this might also cause changes in the position of the centre of gravity. Similar problems occur in industrial control systems, particularly in the chemical industry.

There has consequently been extensive interest in recent years in adaptive, self-optimising, control systems which automatically

optimise their control action despite changes occurring in the system being controlled. Gibson[25] has pointed out the difference between learning systems and adaptive systems. An adaptive system modifies itself in the face of a new environment so as to optimise its performance. A learning system is designed to recognise familiar features and patterns in a situation and then, from its past experience or learned behaviour, it reacts in an optimum manner. In the former, emphasis is placed on reacting to a new situation, while in the latter the emphasis is on remembering and recognising previously-encountered situations. An adaptive system will react in the same way each and every time that a particular situation is encountered, while a learning system will improve its performance each time. Andrew[26] has suggested that while many cybernetic models handle discrete signals, self-optimising adaptive control systems in general operate on continuous signals.

It is not proposed to give here an extensive review of the field of adaptive control systems. Instead, as a typical example, only one particular piece of work which is well known to the writer will be mentioned briefly. P. C. Young[27] has approached the problem of determination of the basic characteristics (or parameters) of a control system in such a form that they can be used to adjust the system to achieve the required performance. This so-called 'Satisfaction-Error Parameter Tracking System' (SEPTS) has been used as the heart of a 'Satisfaction-Error Self-Adaptive Control' (SESAC) system as shown in Fig. 5. The system has been constructed in various forms, incorporating both analogue and digital computers and hybrid combinations of the two. It can be demonstrated that deliberately-imposed changes in the process being

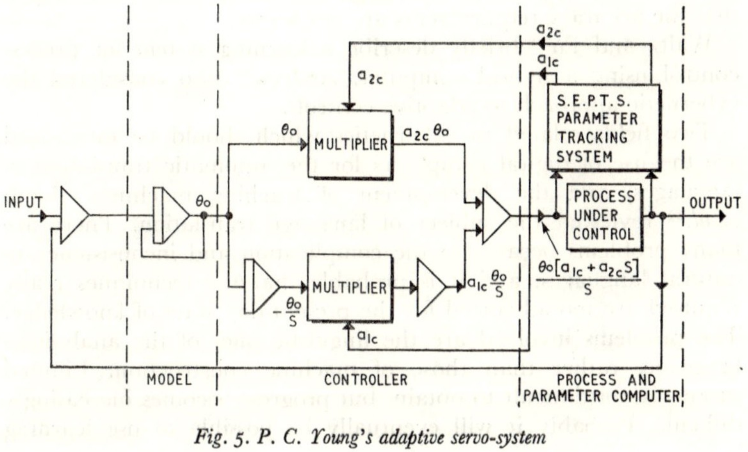

Fig. 5. P. C. Young's adaptive servo-system

controlled are quickly compensated by the adaptive system, the rapid compensation being seen clearly on the recordings of the response of the complete system.

There has been a great deal of other work in the past few years, particularly at universities, on various forms of adaptive control system, though unfortunately little of it has resulted in practical applications. In some cases, very large university departments have been involved, but there would seem to be a gulf between these theoreticians and the real needs of industry. Possibly this is partly because of the erudite manner in which many of the theoreticians prefer to express themselves, though at the same time it must be realised that industry probably does not feel the need for adaptive controls very strongly at present. The present need would seem to be for a more cost-conscious practical approach rather than for more impressive theories.

Crafts[28, 29] asks the question 'What can adaptive machines do that digital computers cannot do?', or 'How can adaptive techniques be used to improve computers?' He answers that, firstly, adaptive machines are advantageous where many inputs are involved because such machines operate on all inputs at the same time ('in parallel'). Secondly, adaptive machines are useful when the statistical description of the data for a problem is unknown or variable, so that fixed system design is not possible. He mentions the case of an adaptive speech-recogniser, which should be capable of recognising a new speaker or a new vocabulary after re-training. Thirdly, because adaptive machines can incorporate unreliable components (e.g. unreliable artificial neurons), they should make good use of modern electronic 'integrated circuits', which show promise of being producible in large numbers at low cost, provided that the accuracy requirements are not severe.

Waltz and Fu[30] briefly describe a learning system for process control using a hybrid computer. Andrew[31] also considered the cybernetic approach to adaptive controls.

Two fields related to cybernetics which should be mentioned are the use of digital computers for the automatic translation of languages, and the development of teaching machines. Booth *et al.*[32] reviewed the subject of language translation. There are many problems because of the complication and inconsistency of natural languages, and it is probable that the techniques really required are too advanced for the present-day state of knowledge. The problems involved are the linguistic ones of the analysis of language, rather than those of machine construction. Limited success is not difficult to obtain, but progress becomes increasingly difficult. Probably it will eventually be possible to use learning

machines for translation, and Olsen *et al.*[33] have demonstrated an elementary application of this possibility.

There are now several different forms of teaching machine on the market. These make use of knowledge of human learning processes and an attempt is made to incorporate some mechanisation by formalising the known processes. Probably the earliest worker in this field was Pressey[34], who exhibited a teaching machine to the American Psychological Association as early as 1925. However, such work did not really gather impetus until after the advent of cybernetics in the 1950's. Pask [35-37] was an early worker in this field. Goodman[38] gives an excellent short introduction to the techniques used. Skinner[39] uses an approach in which the teaching material is divided up into very small segments. When the human student has learned each step, the machine asks a question. The steps are arranged to be so small that the student will almost never give a wrong answer. Another approach is that of Crowder, who developed an idea of Pressey.[40] In this case, the answer given by the student to a multi-choice question determines the next step of instruction. Thus in this case there is feedback from the student to the machine. Teaching machines have proved quite successful in some applications, and books have been written in such a form that they can be used for instruction using the same approach as that used in teaching machines. Skinner's approach is sometimes known as the 'linear' method, while Crowder's approach is called the 'branching' method.

REFERENCES

1. BABCOCK, H. W., 'An Electronic Code Translator', *Electron. Engrng.*, **18**, 282 (1946)
2. HAYTON, T., HUGHES, C. J., and SAUNDERS, R. L., 'Telegraph Codes and Convertors', *Proc. I.E.E.*, **101**, 137 (1954)
3. CARTER, R. O., and WHEELER, L. K., 'Code Convertors for the Interconnection of Morse and Teleprinter Systems', *Proc. I.E.E.*, **101**, 151 (1954)
4. GOLD, B., 'Machine Recognition of Hand-Sent Morse', *Trans. I.R.E.*, **IT5**, 17 (1959)
5. SELFRIDGE, O. G., and NEISSER, U., 'Pattern Recognition by Machine', *Scient. Amer.*, **203**, 60 (1960)
6. SELFRIDGE, O. G., 'Pandemonium; A Paradigm for Learning', *Mechanisation of Thought Processes*, **I**, 513, H.M.S.O. (1959)
7. MCELWAIN, C. K., and EVENS, M. B., 'The Degarbler—A Program for Correcting Machine-Read Morse Code', *Inf. and Contr.*, **5**, 368 (1962)
8. SHEPARD, R. N., 'Analysis of Proximities as a Technique for the Study of Information Processing in Man', *Human Factors*, **8**, 33 (1963)
9. ANON., 'An Experimental Shorthand Transcription Machine', *Proc. Contr. Automat.*, **10**, 335 (1963)
10. KOBRINSKI, A. E., *et al.*, 'Problems of Bio-Electric Control', *Automatic and Remote Control* (Ed. J. F. Coales), 619, Butterworths (1961)
11. TOMOVIC, R., 'The Human Hand as a Feedback System', *ibid.*, 624
12. BOTTOMLEY, A., *et al.*, 'Muscle Substitutes and Myo-Electric Control', *J. Brit. I.R.E.*, **26**, 439 (1963)

13. BOTTOMLEY, A., and COWELL, T., 'An Artificial Hand Controlled by the Nerves', *New Scientist*, **21**, 668 (1964)
14. HORN, W. G., 'Muscle Voltage Moves Artificial Hand', *Electronics*, **36**, 32 (1963)
15. BASMAJIAN, J. V., 'Conscious Control of Single Nerve Cells', *New Scientist*, **20**, 662 (1963)
16. HARRISON, L., 'Paralytic's Brain + Myocoder = Hope', *Electronics*, **37**, 74 (1964)
17. VODOVNIK, L., and MCLEOD, W. D., 'Electronic Detours of Broken Nerve Paths', *Electronics*, **38**, 110 (1965)
18. STARK, L., 'Stability, Oscillations and Noise in the Human Pupil Servomechanism', *Proc. I.R.E.*, **47**, 1925 (1959)
19. KATZNELSON, J., and GOULD, L. A., 'The Design of Non-Linear Filters and Control Systems', *Inf. and Control*, **7**, 117 (1964)
20. STERN, H. J., 'A Simple Method for the Early Diagnosis of Abnormalities of the Pupillary Reaction', *Brit. J. Ophthalm.*, **28**, 275 (1944)
21. CAMPBELL, F. W., and WHITESIDE, T. C. D., 'Induced Pupillary Oscillations', *Brit. J. Ophthalm.*, **34**, 180 (1950)
22. STARK, L., and SHERMAN, P. M., 'A Servo-Analytic Study of Consensual Pupil Reflex to Light', *J. Neurophysiol.*, **20**, 17 (1957)
23. STARK, L., and CORNSWEET, T. N., 'Testing a Servo-Analytic Hypothesis for Pupil Oscillations', *Science*, **127**, 588 (1958)
24. STARK, L., CAMPBELL, F. W., and ATWOOD, J., 'Pupil Unrest; An Example of Noise in a Biological Servomechanism', *Nature*, **182**, 857 (1958)
25. GIBSON, J. E., 'Adaptive Learning Systems', *Proc. N.E.C.*, **18**, 795 (1962)
26. ANDREW, A. M., 'The Utilisation of Environment Continuity by Self-Organising Systems', *Proc. Symp. Math. Theory of Automata.*, 623, Polytechnic (1963)
27. YOUNG, P. C., 'The Determination of the Parameters of a Dynamic Process', *Radio Electron. Engr.*, **29**, 345 (1965)
28. CRAFTS, H. S., 'Components That Learn and How To Use Them', *Electronics*, **36**, 49 (1963)
29. CRAFTS, H. S., 'Design of a Magnetic Variable-Gain Component for Adaptive Networks', *I.E.E.E. Wescon, Pt.* **4**, *Paper* **6.2** (1963)
30. WALTZ, M. D., and FU, K. S., 'A Computer-Simulated Learning Control System', *I.E.E.E. Internat. Conv. Record*, **12** (1), 190 (1964)
31. ANDREW, A. M., 'Self-Optimising Control Mechanisms and Some Principles for More Advanced Learning Machines', *Automatic and Remote Control* (Ed. J. F. Coales), 636, Butterworths (1961)
32. BOOTH, A. D., BRANDWOOD, L., and CLEAVE, J. P., *Mechanical Resolution of Linguistic Problems*, Butterworths (1958)
33. OLSEN, H. F., BELAR, H., and DE SOBRINO, R., 'Demonstration of a Speech-Processing System Consisting of a Speech Analyser, Translator, Typer and Synthesiser', *J.A.S.A.*, **34**, 1535 (1962); (see also p. 166)
34. PRESSEY, S. L., 'A Simple Apparatus Which Gives Tests, and Scores and Teaches', *School and Society*, **23** (1926)
35. PASK, G., 'The Teaching Machine as a Control Mechanism', *Trans. S.I.T.*, **12**, 72 (1960)
36. PASK, G., *An Approach to Cybernetics*, Hutchinson (1961)
37. PASK, G., 'A Discussion of Artificial Intelligence and Self-Organisation', *Advances in Computers*, **5**, 109 (1964)
38. GOODMAN, R., *Programmed Learning and Teaching Machines*, E.U.P. (1962-63)
39. SKINNER, B. F., 'Teaching Machines', *Science*, **128**, 969 (1958)
40. PRESSEY, S. L., 'Development and Appraisal of Devices Providing Automatic Scoring of Objective Tests and Concomitant Self-Instruction', *J. Psychol.*, **49**, 417 (1959)

10

Artificial Nerve Cells

There have been numerous attempts to simulate the actions of neurons and of nervous transmission, using chemical, electrical or electronic means. A widely known early model of nervous transmission is the iron-wire-in-nitric-acid arrangement due to Lillie.[1] Lillie reviewed earlier attempts to simulate nervous transmission and electrolytic 'action at a distance', and he described his own work in this field. He was able to draw astonishing parallels between nervous transmission and the transmission of a wave of chemical activity along an iron wire immersed in nitric acid. The acid oxidises the surface of the iron, leaving a surface coating of oxide which protects the iron from further attack. However, the protecting film can easily be broken down locally by mechanical, electrical, thermal or chemical means, so exposing the underlying iron to a fresh attack by the acid. The iron in this region becomes about 0·7 V positive to the rest of the iron because of the local electrochemical action of the acid. The iron and acid in this region form a local electric battery, and so a local electric current circulates through the iron and the acid. If this local electric current is strong enough, it causes breakdown of the adjacent oxide film, while the acid attack replaces the oxide film in the place at which it was originally removed. In this way, the breakdown propagates along the wire in the form of a dark zone accompanied by local effervescence.

Like nerve fibre, the iron wire model exhibits all-or-none activity. Lillie found that continuous electrical oscillation is possible if the wire is constrained in a glass tube or if a constant electric current is passed through the wire as cathode. He was able to draw numerous other parallels between the activity of his model and that of biological nerve fibre.

Many workers have thought about possible parallels between the action of neon tubes and that of nerve cells. The present writer has

constructed circuits to display by analogy some of the characteristics of biological neurons, using neon lamp oscillators. Walter[2] gave details of a form of artificial nerve fibre using numbers of neon lamps. He criticises Lillie's model on the grounds that the nature of the film in the iron wire model is almost as mysterious as is the nature of natural nerve fibre, and it is not very satisfactory to equate two unknowns. Consequently, Walter uses neon lamps in a criss-cross arrangement in which the normal voltage across each lamp is insufficient to cause it to light. However, if one of the lamps is caused to light by external means, because of its electrical characteristics the voltage across it falls. This change of voltage is coupled in Walter's model to the adjacent lamp in such a way as to cause it to light in its turn. Thus the light is propagated along the line of neon tubes just as an impulse is propagated along nerve fibre. Twenty tubes are used to represent about 5 to 10 cm of frog motor nerve. Walter also showed how to use this model to demonstrate the action of a synapse junction, inhibitory action, etc.

Burns[3] described an electronic model neuron using two thyratron valves. He used this model to test his theories of the operation of certain nerve cells in the brain of the cat. In 1959, Freygang[4] discussed the possible form of an equivalent electrical circuit which would have the same properties as biological nerve fibre. He considered in particular certain nerve cells in the spinal cord of the cat, though he suggested that other nerve cells have similar properties. He gives a form of Hodgkin and Huxley's[5] simple equivalent electrical circuit of the nerve impulse generators, which incorporates two voltage sources (batteries) and two variable resistors. The voltage across the equivalent nerve membrane is caused to vary by the variation of the equivalent circuit resistors. He suggests a simple resistance-capacitance form of electrical transmission line equivalent to the neuron, with voltage pulse generators situated periodically along the line. He also considers the equivalent electrical circuit of the chemically activated pulse generators of the synapses at the nerve end. Moore[6] compares such action with that of transistor switching circuits and shows the form of 'negative-resistance' characteristic obtained, with three possible values of voltage corresponding to some values of current. As mentioned earlier, the shape of the peaked characteristic of current flowing plotted against the voltage across the surface is similar to the surface-effect 'oxygen peaks' which are encountered in polarography.

Artificial nerve cells proposed by Rice[7] were to make use of the properties of colloidal electrolytes. Inhibitory as well as excitatory inputs can be used, though few details are given. Broadly, Rice's

work appears to be a development of the Wehnelt electrolytic interruptor which was widely used early in this century with induction coils; for example, in some of the early spark transmitters for radio. Rice used one electrode of platinum sealed in Pyrex glass, while the other (the cathode) was the aluminium bottle or container. With an electrolyte of saturated ammonium phosphate, this arrangement can give more than 300 electrical oscillations per second when a voltage is applied. Rice's development apparently uses a colloidal gel. With this, a possible density of 1,000 cells per 2 in. cube is claimed, each cell having a memory capability of 15 to 20 hours. As mentioned above, few other details are given.

Chapman[8] used conducting threads of cotton moistened with lime water to connect input stimuli to outputs. Whenever an output occurs due to the presence of a number of inputs, a relatively heavy electrical current is passed through the threads coming from any of the inputs which do not happen to be present at this time, so tending to inhibit their future action. The 'forgetting' process involves a careful control of vapour pressure to determine the rate of evaporation. Pask[9-11] discusses possible physical methods of learning, and describes his own work on an elementary machine for growing, for example, iron threads in ferrous sulphate solution. When discussing Pask's work, MacKay has mentioned the practical difficulties encountered in the course of his own work with silver threads in silver nitrate. Stewart[12] mentions very briefly an electrochemical assembly based on the iron wire model. Crafts[13] describes several devices. In the Memistor, the electrical resistance of a metallic resistor contained in an electrolyte is changed by electroplating from a nearby anode. The amplitude and polarity of the voltage applied to the anode determines the rate of plating or deplating of the resistor, and so varies its electrical resistance. It is possible to obtain a hundred-to-one change of resistance in this way. Widrow *et al.*[14] describes the successful use of the Memistor electrochemical unit in the Madaline assembly which will be discussed later.

Crafts also applied a second-harmonic type of magnetic variable-gain electronic device to the Adaline arrangement. This device has the advantage of low cost. Crafts shows its use in classifying a mixed collection of four-bit binary numbers into four separate categories. Brain[15] used magnetic iron cores with a number of holes, while others have used simpler magnetic cores in adaptive memory schemes. Bray[16] describes opto-electronic-magnetic artificial neurons. In these, electroluminescent lamps form the input elements, and these control the amount of light falling on to photo-electric cells. Integration of the total quantity of light falling on to the photo-electric cells is performed with magnetic 'transfluxor' devices. Such

artificial neurons are small enough for fabrication into reasonably complex yet compact arrays to be possible. Various forms of artificial neurons have been used in the perceptron programme. Palmieri and Sanna[17] have described a bi-stable photosensitive unit for use with the PAPA probabilistic automatic programmer-analyser pattern recognition device.

Crane[18] described a form of artificial nerve cell which he later produced using electromechanical relays. In 1962 he carried out a partial review of the field[19]. He emphasises the problem of size and he points out that attenuation of the signal is avoided in the nerve axon by continuous regeneration of the signal as it travels along. This can be compared with the action of a chemical fuse except that the axon can be used over and over again, provided only that a few milliseconds are allowed for recovery after an impulse has passed. This action, he says, is like a forest fire, since in that case the trees can grow again. In order to achieve this transmission-without-attenuation, energy must be available to the fibre everywhere along its length. Crane gives the name 'Neuristor' to artificial nerve fibres and proceeds to review a number of different forms.

Crane summarises the characteristics of neural transmission as follows.

1. The form of the propagating nervous signal depends only on the nature of the nerve fibre and not on the means by which the signal is started.
2. After an impulse has passed, a short recovery (or refractory) time is required before the next impulse can pass.
3. If separate discharges start from opposite ends of a fibre, they are mutually destructive when they meet (collide), since each leaves behind a refractory region through which neither impulse can continue to propagate.
4. There can be no reflection of a signal when it reaches the end of a neural transmission line, because of the refractory region behind it. In a normal electrical transmission line, on the contrary, reflection can occur at the end of the line in many cases. This produces a secondary signal in the reverse direction in the electrical case, which is not encountered in the neural case.

After discussing various forms of neural junction which can occur, Crane considers a number of practical forms which artificial nerve fibres can take. To replace the neon tube negative-resistance elements used earlier, he discusses the use of solid-state tunnel diodes, four-layer diodes, etc. He makes the point that a decade or two ago this approach of distributing active elements throughout a network would have been considered impractical. Other people who have tried a similar approach include Nagumo *et al.*,[20] who

used tunnel diodes to produce a form of Hodgkin and Huxley's model. They show how signals greater than a given threshold value are amplified, while smaller pulses are attenuated to extinction during transmission. In this way, interfering signals, such as electrical 'noise', are eliminated provided that they have a small amplitude. On the other hand, very large signals are also reduced, but in this case only to a standard size and not to extinction. In a similar way, they showed that the width of a transmitted pulse is increased as it travels along the artificial nerve fibre if the pulse-width is initially too narrow, while it is decreased if the pulse is initially too wide. Their artificial nerve could carry pulses in either direction, and there was mutual extinction if two oppositely-directed pulses met.

Other workers in this field include Yoshizawa *et al.*[21] who use tunnel diodes, Cote[22] who uses four-layer semiconductor diodes, and Rosengreen[23] who uses four-layer semiconductor devices specially fabricated in a solid chain arrangement. Low[24] mentions several different neuron analogues which have been used.

Harmon[25] described a form of artificial neuron incorporating four transistors as shown in Fig. 6. This does not take the form of a

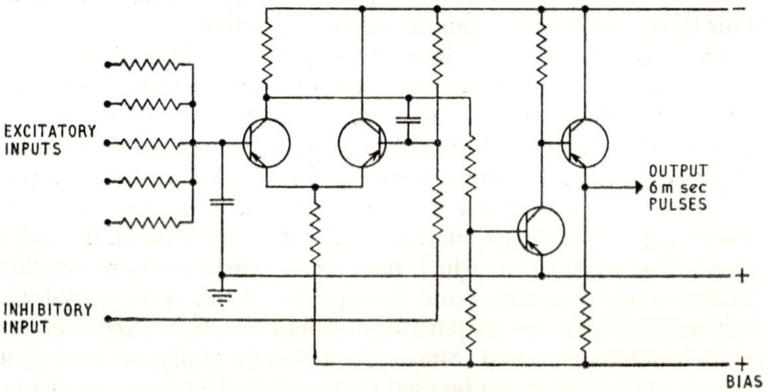

Fig. 6. Harmon's artificial neuron

neural transmission line, but it is designed to display various features of the operation of nerve cells. It has features such as:

Inhibition (there is one inhibitory input).

Excitation and threshold (the five excitatory inputs must supply more than a given total energy within a given time in order to produce an output).

Refractory period (immediately after firing, the neuron cannot fire again for several milliseconds, then it slowly recovers in the next few tens of milliseconds).

Summation (two excitatory inputs occurring a millisecond or so

apart can fire the neuron even though neither on its own could do so).

Harmon *et al.*[26] point out that although the voltages appearing in their models are several orders of magnitude greater than those found in nature, the ratios (for example, the ratio of resting threshold voltage to output pulse voltage level) have been preserved, while biological time constants are also reproduced. Later, Harmon[27] described improved models, and criticised much of the model neuron work which had been reported on the grounds that the model neurons were not precise. However, Brain, replying, pointed out that progress in flying machines had not come from mere slavish copying of biological methods.

McGrogan[28] discusses the characteristics and circuitry of improved neuron models using transistors. In these models, the design is intended to avoid effects caused by variations in or ageing of the transistors. He makes the point that closely controlled characteristics of the individual neurons are essential if experimental work with large numbers is to yield really useful information. Pritsker[29] briefly describes the circuit of a 'flexible-logic' unit having four stable states, any of which can be inhibited by an inhibitor input. This inhibiting memory can be erased if required.

There has been much interest in the so-called majority-logic form of circuit for use in digital computers. Akers and Rutter[30] have listed some of the various names which have been applied to such devices. These include threshold logic, linearly-separable functions, majority decision functions, linear decision functions, linear-input functions, vote-taking functions and weighted-decision functions. They suggest that the popularity of the names decreases in the order given. Two other terms which have been widely used are Adaline (adaptive linear element) and Perceptron A unit. A majority-logic arrangement gives an output if more than a certain fixed number of its inputs are excited. Since this action is similar to that of a neuron, such devices can be used in neural analogue arrangements. Minnick[31] had discussed methods of building such devices, using magnetic cores, transistors, tunnel diodes or electromechanical relays. More recently, Nagy[32] has also discussed possible devices.

The mathematical theory of such elements has been considered by many, including Von Neumann[33] who showed how majority-logic could improve the reliability of neural transmission. Winder[34] gave a short review of work in this field. Many other workers have considered the theory and properties of majority-logic devices, and this might well be a field in which cybernetic thinking can affect the future design of digital computers. One of the problems encountered has been the limitations on the permissible number of

inputs to each device, imposed because of the effects of possible variations in operating conditions. This limitation has been realised since the early days of industrial static-switching equipment, and it has restricted the range of applications of threshold-type switching devices, such as the magnetic amplifier equipment described by Morgan[35]. However, recently Coates and Lewis[36] have described the use of units capable of operating with as many as 15 separate inputs. Dertouzos[37] deals at length with the theory of threshold logic, and he also gives a brief review of the prior theoretical work.

REFERENCES

1. LILLIE, R. S., 'The Passive Iron-Wire Model of Protoplasmic and Nervous Transmission and its Physical Analogies', *Biol. Rev.*, **11**, 181 (1936)
2. WALTER, W. G., *The Living Brain*, Duckworth (1953)
3. BURNS, B. D., 'The Mechanism of After-Bursts in the Cerebral Cortex', *J. Physiol.*, **127**, 168 (1955)
4. FREYGANG, W. H., 'Some Functions of Nerve Cells in Terms of an Equivalent Network', *Proc. I.R.E.*, **47**, 1862 (1959)
5. HODGKIN, A. L., and HUXLEY, A. F., 'A Quantitative Description of Membrane Current and its Application to Conduction and Excitation in Nerve', *J. Physiol.*, **117**, 500 (1952)
6. MOORE, J. W., 'Electronic Control of Some Active Bio-Electric Membranes', *Proc. I.R.E.*, **47**, 1869 (1959)
7. RICE, R. J., 'Simulation of Nerve Cells by Electro-Chemical Methods', *Brit. Comm. Electron.*, **6**, 846 (1959)
8. CHAPMAN, B. L. M., 'A Self-Organising Classifying System', *Cybernetica*, **2**, 152 (1959)
9. PASK, G., 'Physical Analogues to the Growth of a Concept', *Mechanisation of Thought Processes*, **II**, 877, H.M.S.O. (1959)
10. PASK, G., 'The Natural History of Networks', *Self-Organising Systems* (Eds M. C. Yovits and S. Cameron), 232, Pergamon (1960)
11. PASK, G., *An Approach to Cybernetics*, Hutchinson (1961)
12. STEWART, J. L., 'Limits to Animal Discrimination and Recognition in a Noise-Free External Environment', *Trans. I.E.E.E.*, **Mil 7**, 116 (1963)
13. CRAFTS, H. S., 'Components that Learn and How to Use Them', *Electronics*, **36**, 49 (1963)
14. WIDROW, B., *et al.*, 'Practical Applications for Adaptive Data-Processing Systems', *I.E.E.E. Wescon. Record, Pt.* 7, (1963)
15. BRAIN, A. E., 'The Simulation of Neural Elements by Electrical Networks Based on Multi-Aperture Magnetic Cores', *Proc. I.R.E.*, **49**, 49 (1961)
16. BRAY, T. E., 'An Opto-Electronic-Magnetic Neuron Component'., *Proc. N.E.C.*, **17**, 322 (1961)
17. PALMIERI, G., and SANNA, R., 'Light-to-Light Discriminator Switch', *Supp. Nuovo Cimento*, **19**, 91 (1961)
18. CRANE, H. D., 'The Neuristor', *Trans. I.R.E.*, **EC9**, 370 (1960)
19. CRANE, H. D., 'Neuristor—A Novel Device and System Concept', *Proc. I.R.E.*, **50**, 2048 (1962)
20. NAGUMO, J., ARIMOTO, S., and YOSHIZAWA, S., 'An Active Pulse Transmission Line Simulating the Nerve Axon', *Proc. I.R.E.*, **50**, 2061 (1962)
21. YOSHIZAWA, S., *et al.*, 'An Active Pulse Transmission Line', *Electr. Commun. Japan*, **46**, 22 (1963)

22. COTE, A. J., 'A Neuristor Prototype', *Proc. I.R.E.*, **49**, 1430 (1961)
23. ROSENGREEN, A., 'Experimental Neuristor Gives Nerve-Like Pulse Propagation', *Electronics*, **36**, 25 (1963)
24. LOW, P. R., 'Influence of Component Imperfections on Performance of Trainable Systems', *I.E.E.E. Wescon, Pt.* 4 (1963)
25. HARMON, L. D., 'The Artificial Neuron', *Science*, **129**, 962 (1959)
26. HARMON, L. D., *et al.*, 'Analog Models of Neural Mechanism', *Trans. I.R.E.*, **IT8**, 107 (1962)
27. HARMON, L. D., 'Neural Analogs', *Proc. I.R.E.*, **49**, 1316 (1961)
28. MCGROGAN, E. P., 'Improved Transistor Neuron Models', *Proc. N.E.C.*, **17**, 302 (1961)
29. PRITSKER, B. S., 'A Teachable Logic Machine', *Autom. Rem. Contr.*, **23**, 781 (1962)
30. AKERS, S. B., and RUTTER, B. H., 'The Use of Threshold Logic in Pattern Recognition', *I.E.E.E. Wescon, Pt. 4* (1963)
31. MINNICK, R. C., 'Linear-Input Logic', *Trans. I.R.E.*, **EC10**, 6 (1961)
32. NAGY, G. J., 'Adaptive Devices and Systems', *Electro-Technol.*, **77**, 40 (1966)
33. VON NEUMANN, J., 'Probabilistic Logics and the Synthesis of Reliable Organisms from Unreliable Components', *Automata Studies* (Eds C. E. Shannon and J. McCarthy), 43, Princeton (1956)
34. WINDER, R. O., 'Some Recent Papers in Threshold Logic', *Proc. I.R.E.*, **49**, 1100 (1961)
35. MORGAN, R. E., 'The Biased-Rectifier Amplifier: A Pulse Magnetic Amplifier', *Trans. A.I.E.E.*, **73**, Pt. 1, 584 (1954)
36. COATES, C. L., and LEWIS, P. M., 'Donut, A Threshold Gate Computer', *Trans. I.E.E.E.*, **EC13**, 240 (1964)
37. DERTOUZOS, M. L., *Threshold Logic, A Synthesis Approach*, M.I.T. (1965)

11

Neuron Assemblies

As seen in the previous chapter, it is not too difficult to simulate the known properties of individual nerve cells and fibres in various ways. However, the problem of assembling networks (or nets) of artificial neurons on a biological scale is at present beyond the bounds of known technology (and finance). Consequently, practical studies in this field have of necessity involved quite limited assemblies. Theoretical studies have, perhaps, been less inhibited, though it is not easy to evaluate the real importance of such work. For example, most of us have difficulty in visualising extensive three-dimensional arrays of assorted objects. Probably for this reason, many of the studies have limited themselves to two dimensions, i.e. to a flat plane array of neurons, though without always making it clear that this immediately renders the study completely artificial. There has nevertheless been extensive work in this direction, particularly during the past decade.

As part of a biological study, Rashevsky[1] considered the action of nerve nets, and he suggested how arrangements of the inhibitory and excitatory connections of nerve cells could produce various logical operations. In addition, he suggested that perhaps short-term memory involved recirculating information, in the form of pulses, around loops in nervous pathways, a suggestion which has even now not been adequately resolved. Lettvin *et al.*[2] found some support for Rashevsky in their studies of the nervous mechanism in the retina of the frog's eye.

McCulloch and Pitts[3] used Boolean logical algebra to consider the activity of neural networks, and so they opened the way for the application to the study of the nervous system of the engineering knowledge which would shortly be acquired in the course of work on electronic computer systems. In 1947, Pitts and McCulloch[4] suggested a possible way in which an array of simple nerve cells

could be used to compare an input pattern with a pattern stored in a memory arrangement. However, such a system has not yet been discovered in biological networks. Making the point that our computers are at a very low level of complexity compared with biological systems, McCulloch[5] compared the early digital computer ENIAC, which used 10,000 electronic valves, with the nervous system of a flatworm.

McCulloch has adopted the descriptive term 'anastomosis' to illustrate the way in which, in the nervous system, afferent sensory nerves run together, like tributaries towards the main stream of a river, and then, after combining and mixing together their information in the central nervous system (as the tributary waters mix in the main stream of a river), they branch out into the 'delta' of the efferent nervous system.

Hebb[6] suggested that permanent changes in the strengths of the synaptic junctions on nerve cells constitute the biological methods of permanent memory. He also suggested that the axon of one cell can fire another cell if it happens to be close enough, and that, if this happens repeatedly, a growth process takes place tending to increase the efficiency of the process and so making the action more likely in the future. It should be mentioned that it has sometimes been suggested that perhaps the process of learning involves instead the inhibition of incorrect responses. Milner[7] and Pribram[8] have elaborated on Hebb's ideas. Their work is reviewed briefly by George,[9] who also discusses much other work in this field.

Burns[10] carried out experiments on part of the cortex of a cat. The part was isolated from the rest of the cortex completely except for its blood supply. He found that alpha rhythms no longer existed, but that activity did spread out from any point at which it was initiated by an external stimulus. He suggested a possible flat, two-dimensional array of neurons, which includes rings, around which excitation can circulate repeatedly. Based on this, he carried out further work which appeared to verify the suggestion. Burks and Wright[11] have also discussed the theory of neural nets.

The work of McCulloch and Pitts has been extended theoretically by Kleene,[12] who attempted a simplification of the theoretical derivation of some of their results. Von Neumann[13] notes that, unlike normal logical theory, the theory of neural networks must include a consideration of both time and sequence, because later actions depend in part on earlier events. He continues to consider methods of reducing the number of different types of nerve unit which must be considered, and then discusses the effect of unreliable neurons. However, he points out that it is dangerous to identify the real physical (or biological) world with the models which are

constructed to explain it. He suggests that even plausible explanations of nervous reaction should be taken with a very large grain of salt. Copi *et al.*[14] gave a further simplified version of Kleene's analysis.

Burns[15] assembled a network of his thyratron model neurons. He found that the behaviour of the model network proved similar to that of certain neurons in the cat in every way tested. Culbertson[16] considers the theoretical capabilities of 'complete' robots in which it is assumed that there is no limit to the number of cells which can be used. His assumption is that it will be possible to impose practical limitations later. He discusses how the action of a 'memoryless' robot can get into an ever-repeating chain sequence if an aim cannot be achieved, attempts to achieve the aim being repeated for ever. This possibility is avoided if there is an element of probability in the action of the robot, since then at some time the robot will make the 'wrong' action and so escape from the repeating circle of events. He suggests that, at the whim of its designer, the complete robot such as he discusses might, for example, speak no German at all until it was triggered by the one word, say, 'schnell', but from then on it would speak perfect German.

Allanson[17] has considered the properties which would be expected of a network of idealised neurons connected together at random. He denies the possibility that neural time delays are used in recoding temporal information into spatial form. His argument does not consider the inverse possibility discussed by Scott and Williams.[18] Allanson dismisses the possibility by calculating the large number of neurons required to provide an extremely long time delay of 10 sec, but he does not justify this choice of time. He suggests that instead there is perhaps an almost-oscillatory network, the function of which is to transform temporal to spatial patterns. He cites the alpha rhythm as possible evidence of the existence of his almost-oscillating network. However, he also mentions that it is quite possible that all of his suggestions are equally erroneous. Smith and Davidson[19] followed up the work of Allanson[17] and others with an investigation using a digital computer programme. They found some similarity with the physiological results of Burns[10] on the cortex of a cat.

Beurle[20, 21] has discussed possible methods by which the brain stores and uses information. He points out that it is probable that the brain achieves complex control of the body by combining simple sub-routines as is done in a digital computer. Consequently we do not have to look for a complicated basic process in the brain. He considers the properties to be expected from a randomly-connected mass of cells having properties similar to the known properties of neurons. He assumes that the probability of connection between

pairs of neurons falls off with distance, basing this assumption on the known decrease in density of the fibres of a neuron with distance from the cell nucleus. He mentions, however, that in fact our knowledge of cortical organisation is still pathetically small, being based mainly on the properties of neurons outside the cortex.

Beurle used a digital computer to simulate the action of a flat two-dimensional array of such cells, pointing out that the results must be interpreted as giving only a general diagrammatic indication of what might be expected in a large three-dimensional array. It was possible to demonstrate how neural activity could spread out from a centre where a number of cells have been simultaneously activated, so producing a large over-all stimulating effect. A small stimulus, on the other hand, produced no reaction at all. He also considered the stabilising effect of mutual inhibition, though he notes that there is no direct evidence for its occurrence in the cortex. He assumed that the sensitivity of individual cells can increase slightly each time that they are activated, and that this leads to learning behaviour. He proceeded to construct block diagrams of the way in which he felt that short-term and long-term memories might possibly act and interact.

Farley and Clark[22] did very similar work to that of Beurle, also using a digital computer. They assumed that neurons exist in a flat sheet and that the probability that any pair of cells are connected falls as the distance between them increases. The properties of a 36 x 36 square array of 1,296 cells were investigated, the number of connections per cell being between 10 and 30. They compare their work with that of Beurle.

Taylor[23] considered the effects of mutual inhibition in a two-dimensional array of cells, and he was able to demonstrate a contrast-enhancement effect. Another feature was that when an artificial neuron was stimulated by two nerve inputs having different pulse frequencies, smooth curves of output frequency against one of the input frequencies were obtained, rather than the fluctuating curves which might be expected as the input impulses go in and out of step. Taylor explains the unexpected smoothness of the curves as a beneficial effect of electrical noise (i.e. random fluctuations), and he suggests that such an effect might be present in the animal nervous system. In this connection, it is interesting to note the beneficial effects of fluctuations in visual systems which will be mentioned again in the next chapter. In 1957, Taylor described a low-pass electrical filter designed to simulate the transformation from nerve action-potential to post-synaptic potential which occurs when a nerve impulse travelling along the axon of one neuron arrives at a second neuron and tends either to increase or to decrease its firing

frequency. In 1962, Taylor[24] attempted to find a theory of learning which does not conflict with existing knowledge. He mentioned the importance of the frontal lobes and suggested possible reasons for the absence from them of significant electrical activity. He suggested a form of neural organisation suitable for analogue computer testing. Again, in 1964, Taylor[25] suggested a possible way in which the neurons are organised in the cortex.

Rochester *et al.*[26] attempted to mechanise Hebb's theories of nervous activity and brain assembly by using a digital computer to simulate assemblies first of 69 and then of 512 neurons. The speed of operation was scaled down to be 7,600 times slower than that of biological systems. They were able to demonstrate a somewhat oscillatory form of short-term memory. Neurons were assumed to decay slowly whenever they were not activated. Later, some inhibition of cells was introduced. Although not entirely successful, this investigation prepared the way for further work.

Braitenberg *et al.*[27] briefly discuss the properties to be expected from a system of oscillators coupled together. From a number of predicted properties, the outstanding one is that of producing the known characteristics of the alpha rhythm. Goldstein[28] considers the theoretical response to be expected from a mass of neural elements, each contributing its own elemental waveform. He points out that this mass-response is all that one can expect to detect from the cortex with practical 'gross' pick-up electrodes. His investigation was suggested by the fact that repeated presentations of a stimulus do not produce identical responses, despite all efforts to maintain identical conditions. Willis[29] considers the properties of an assembly of 'plastic' neurons, in which the threshold depends on the past history of the cell. He simulated an assembly of 288 such neurons on a computer.

McCulloch[30] shows theoretically how networks of idealised neurons can give reliable results although built from unreliable parts. Minsky and Selfridge[31] feel that it is over-optimistic to expect that the complexities and function of a random net of nerve cells might enable it to solve really hard problems. They consider various organised or ordered networks of neurons and they suggest that the results achieved by random networks would be worse. Random nets might be useful in small local tasks such as correlating or classifying inputs, but more complex behaviour should not be expected.

Caianiello[32] considers mathematically, yet using surprisingly few symbols, the theory of neuron assemblies. He emphasises that his theoretical model is intended to simulate the physiology of neurons in their normal condition and environment in the living tissue. He suggests that experiments on isolated neurons are as irrelevant to

the study of the collective behaviour of neuron assemblies as are the radiation spectra of sodium and chlorine to the crystal structure of common salt. He feels that his theory has many other applications, such as the prediction of stock-exchange trends, feminine fashions, etc.

Josephson *et al.*[33] have studied the nerve nets of sea creatures such as jellyfish. They simulated flat two-dimensional nets of 32 x 32 and of 100 x 100 cells on digital computers. Provision was made for simultaneous stimulation of many elements, since this is inevitable in experiments with live cells because of the relatively large size of any stimulating electrode compared with that of a neuron. The computer was supplied with the 'address' of each neuronal junction to be stimulated, and it then produced a list of the cells which would be stimulated in turn by the first neurons after a certain time interval. The process was then repeated over and over, to examine the way in which excitation spreads.

Arbib[34] discussed the theoretical equivalence of neural nets to finite automata and Turing machines. McGrogan[35] tried to improve the reliability of transistorised artificial neurons, even at the expense of increased amplification and cost, since reliability of the individual cell is much more important in investigations involving small nets of 100 or so neurons than it is in the immensely larger biological networks. The characteristics of four-transistor devices are given. Maron[36] simulated 10 neurons with 200 synaptic connections on a digital computer. It was then tested as a learning and predicting machine using the probability theory of Reicherback. Nagumo[37] partially reviewed the field of work on neural nets. Bernhard[38] based his discussion of a possible neural network model on suggestions published by Sigmund Freud. Dertouzos[39] considers the theory of neuron-like devices alone and in combination.

REFERENCES

1. RASHEVSKY, N., *Mathematical Biophysics*, University of Chicago Press (1938)
2. LETTVIN, J. Y., *et al.*, 'What the Frog's Eye Tells the Frog's Brain', *Proc. I.R.E.*, **47**, 1940 (1959)
3. MCCULLOCH, W. S., and PITTS, W. A., 'A Logical Calculus of the Ideas Immanent in Nervous Activity', *Bull. Math. Biophys.*, **5**, 115 (1943)
4. PITTS., W. A., and MCCULLOCH, W. S., 'How We Know Universals: The Perception of Auditory and Visual Forms', *Bull. Math. Biophys.*, **9**, 127 (1947)
5. MCCULLOCH, W. S., 'The Brain as a Computing Machine', *Electrical Eng.*, **68**, 492 (1949)
6. HEBB, D. O., *The Organisation of Behaviour; A Neuro-Physiological Theory*, Wiley (1949)
7. MILNER, P. M., 'The Cell Assembly, Mk. 2', *Psychol. Rev.*, **64**, 242 (1957)
8. PRIBRAM, K. H., 'A Review of Theory in Physiological Psychology', *Ann. Rev. Psych.*, **11**, 1 (1960)

9. GEORGE, F. H., *The Brain as a Computer*, Pergamon (1961)
10. BURNS, B. D., 'Some Properties of Isolated Cerebral Cortex in the Unanaesthetised Cat', *J. Physiol.*, **112**, 156 (1951)
11. BURKS, A. W., and WRIGHT, J. B., 'Theory of Logical Nets', *Proc. I.R.E.*, **41**, 1357 (1953)
12. KLEENE, S. C., 'Representation of Events in Nerve Nets and Finite Automata', *Automata Studies* (Eds C. E. Shannon and J. McCarthy), Princeton, 3 (1956)
13. VON NEUMANN, J., 'Probabilistic Logics and the Synthesis of Reliable Organisms from Unreliable Components', *Automata Studies* (Eds C. E. Shannon and J. McCarthy), Princeton, 43 (1956)
14. COPI, I. M., *et al.*, 'Realisation of Events by Logical Nets', *J.A.C.M.*, **5**, 181 (1958)
15. BURNS, B. D., 'The Mechanism of After-Bursts in the Cerebral Cortex', *J. Physiol.*, **127**, 168 (1955)
16. CULBERTSON, J. T., 'Some Uneconomical Robots', *Automata Studies* (Eds C. E. Shannon and J. McCarthy), Princeton, 99 (1956)
17. ALLANSON, J. T., 'Some Properties of a Randomly Connected Neural Network', *Information Theory* (Ed. C. Cherry), Butterworths, 303 (1956)
18. SCOTT, P., and WILLIAMS, K. G., 'A Note on Temporal Coding as a Mechanism in Sensory Perception', *Inf. Control*, **2**, 380 (1959)
19. SMITH, D. R., and DAVIDSON, C. H., 'Maintained Activity in Neural Nets', *J.A.C.M.*, **9**, 268 (1962)
20. BEURLE, R. L., 'Properties of a Mass of Cells Capable of Regenerating Pulses', *Phil. Trans. Roy. Soc.*, **240B**, 55 (1956)
21. BEURLE, R. L., 'Storage and Manipulation of Information in the Brain', *J.I.E.E.*, **5**, 75 (1959)
22. FARLEY, B. G., and CLARKE, W. A., 'Activity in Networks of Neuron-Like Elements', *Information Theory* (Ed. C. Cherry), Butterworths, 242 (1961)
23. TAYLOR, W. K., 'Electrical Simulation of Some Nervous System Functional Activities', *Information Theory* (Ed. C. Cherry), Butterworths, 314 (1956)
24. TAYLOR, W. K., 'The Theory of Cortical Organisation and of Learning', *Trans. I.R.E.*, **IT8**, S144 (1962)
25. TAYLOR, W. K., 'Cortico-Thalamic Organisation and Memory', *Proc. Roy. Soc.*, **159B**, 466 (1964)
26. ROCHESTER, N., *et al.*, 'Tests on a Cell-Assembly Theory of the Action of the Brain Using a Large Digital Computer', *Trans, I.R.E.* **IT2**, 80 (1956)
27. BRAITENBERG, V., *et al.*, 'Systems of Coupled Oscillators as Functional Models of Neuronal Assemblies', *Nuovo Cimento*, **11**, 278 (1959)
28. GOLDSTEIN, M. H., 'A Statistical Model for Interpreting Neuro-Electric Responses', *Inf. Control*, **3**, 1 (1960)
29. WILLIS, D. G., 'Plastic Neurons as Memory Elements', *I.R.E. Wescon*, **3**, (4), 55 (1959)
30. MCCULLOCH, W. S., 'The Reliability of Biological Systems', *Self-Organising Systems* (Eds M. C. Yovits and S. Cameron), Pergamon, 262 (1960)
31. MINSKY, M., and SELFRIDGE, O. G., 'Learning in Random Nets', *Information Theory*, 1960 (Ed. C. Cherry), Butterworths (1961)
32. CAIANIELLO, E. R., 'Outline of a Theory of Thought-Processes and Thinking Machines', *J. Theoret. Biol.*, **1**, 204 (1961)
33. JOSEPHSON, R. K., *et al.*, 'A Simulation Study of a Diffuse Conducting System Based on Coelenterate Nerve Nets', *J. Theoret. Biol.*, **1**, 460 (1961)
34. ARBIB, M., 'Turing Machines, Finite Automata and Neural Nets', *J.A.C.M.*, **8**, 467 (1961)
35. MCGROGAN, E. P., 'Improved Transistor Neuron Models', *Proc. N.E.C.*, **17**, 302 (1961)

36. MARON, M. E., 'Design Principles for an Intelligent Machine', *Trans. I.R.E.*, **IT8**, S179 (1962)
37. NAGUMO, J., 'Neural Nets and Their Use in Simulation of the Brain', *Electr. Commun. Japan*, **46**, 82 (1963)
38. BERNHARD, R., 'Towards a Chemical Kinetic Brain Model', *J. Theoret. Biol.*, **6**, 244 (1964)
39. DERTOUZOS, M. L., *Threshold Logic, A Synthesis Approach*, M.I.T. (1965)

12

Visual Pattern Recognition

Possibly more attention has been given, all over the world, to the field of visual pattern recognition than to any other subdivision of cybernetics. Some of the impetus for this has come from the computer industry, since it would be useful if digital computers could react to written numbers, letters and symbols without the necessity for a human to transcribe the information into special computer language and symbols. In some cases the usefulness has been exaggerated. For instance, many cheques are now marked with information such as the national number of the bank branch in characters which can be read as easily by certain computers as by a human. However, as the writer has pointed out,[1] since the human could easily read the same information in normal typescript elsewhere on the same cheque, the utility of the dual-purpose script in this case is not immediately apparent.

Nevertheless, work like this can be of importance to cybernetics, especially when it leads to machines which can learn to classify visual patterns and so make use of the differences between one and another. However, there has been so much work in this field in the past few years that it is difficult to achieve more than a superficial review here. As early as 1916, Flower[2] proposed a typewriter which would automatically read printed letters and type them. The printed letter was to be projected on to an array of selenium photocells. By superimposing all possible letters, it was hoped that the light areas individual to any one letter could be discovered, so that these could be used for recognition of that particular pattern.

Glovazky[3] showed that if there are C cells in the retina, and only P different patterns have to be recognised, then a total number $(C-P+1)$ of the cells are redundant. Riekeman[4] discussed this further, and later Gill[5] described a method of reducing the scanning required of a visual pattern recogniser which has only to differentiate

between a fixed small number of patterns. In 1957, Greanias[6] used a programmed digital computer to recognise characters having a fixed size and shape, Chow[70] discussed the theory of character recognition based on the use of conditional probability, and Dimond[49] developed a process for reading hand-printed numerals drawn in accordance with certain constraints on size, proportion and location.

Taylor[7] considered possible reasons for apparent movement seen in some optical illusions (MacKay[8]). He suggested that possibly the apparent movement is caused by a combination with adaptation of the mutual inhibition of retinal cells which appears to be a feature of contrast enhancement. This mutual inhibition was seen in the results of Lettvin *et al.*,[9] which is an example of biological investigation guided by prior engineering work on pattern recognition. They found that the nerve signals sent from the retina of the frog to its cortex are independent of the general level of illumination. The image is expressed neurally in terms of local sharp edges and contrasts, curvature of dark edges, movement and rapid local changes of illumination. Hartline[10] mentions that receptor cells can respond to a wide range of illumination since they have a logarithmic response, and yet they can respond vigorously to very small sudden changes of illumination. He points out that there is interaction between neurons in the retina, each receptor being inhibited by its neighbours. Unfortunately, some investigators go to great lengths to attempt the explanation of human pattern recognition while completely ignoring this elementary fact of retinal contrast enhancement. Some suggest that perhaps this method is not used in higher animals.

In addition to this contrast enhancement by mutual inhibition, minute tremors of the eye muscles also have the effect of enhancing contrast. In fact it was shown by Riggs *et al.*[11] that if the effect of these tremors is removed, a form of neural fatigue sets in and objects just disappear from view. It is interesting to note that Kapany[12] has discussed investigations of optical systems using bundles of glass fibres, in which it has been found that tremor at the sending end can reduce background 'noise' caused by the discrete nature of the fibres, and so it can improve the picture at the receiving end.

Unger[13] distinguishes between pattern detection and pattern recognition. The former entails sorting a number of patterns into sets. The latter entails the identification of a single pattern as one of several known classes. Any recognition problem can be considered as a finite number of detection problems, though the converse is not true. He simulated the spatial computer SPAC (Unger[14]), which comprises a rectangular array of logic units, on a digital

computer. This made the recognition process rather slow, though quite successful. Greene[15] gives 'sketchy proposals' for applying quantum theoretical methods to pattern recognition, his suggestion being that perception is the first part of the process of recognition.

Murray[19] reviews the 'perceptron' programme originated by the psychologist Rosenblatt,[16-18] concentrating his review on the engineering aspects. He feels that there is reason to believe that such a machine might eventually be useful, particularly in the detection and interpretations of signals in a noisy background, in the automation of heuristic problems such as military tactical command, and in the control loops of adaptive servomechanisms. Murray points out that, with the machines discussed, the loss or malfunction of a few components is not likely noticeably to affect the reliability of operation. Perhaps we should comment here that the same is true of an automatic telephone exchange, which in biological terms has a purely 'reflex' action. The perceptron (Rosenblatt insists that we must use a small 'p') includes S— or sensory units, A— or association units and a relatively small number of R— or response units (output units). Each sensory unit has several outputs which are manually connected at random to association units, some of the connections being excitatory and others inhibitory. The association units similarly control response units, and some of the outputs from response units are fed back to adjust the operating-threshold levels of the association units. This gives the device a memory and adaptive capability. The feedback reinforces any units causing a particular response, while it inhibits those units actively opposing the response, though the maximum amount of feedback is limited in order to prevent instability. In one scheme, the total signal feedback from any given output is constant, but it is only divided between those association units which are actively causing this particular output to appear. The other units then receive no feedback signal at this time.

In general, optical sensory units have been considered with the perceptron, though other forms of sensory unit could, in principle, be used. Murray points out that association units do not die or reproduce, and in this they are unlike the equivalent biological cells. The use of inhibitory as well as of excitatory connections makes it possible for the perceptron to give different responses to two patterns, one of which is part of the other, provided that the smaller pattern excites some association units which are inhibited by the larger pattern.

Maximum values and forgetting delays are introduced to maintain flexibility with time and to permit adaptation to new factors in the environment. The perceptron was simulated on a digital

computer. It could discriminate between E's and X's regardless of the orientation of the letters. In other experiments the perceptron learned to distinguish between E's and F's using inhibition, and, if rotation was eliminated, between squares and diamonds. Rosenblatt[17] discusses some of the theory of the perceptron. Beer, in his discussion, criticises much of this paper, stating that 'since it does not actually say anything, there was no need to write it', though it does 'build up an ethos of potency around the perceptron'. Rosenblatt uses even more extensive symbolism in his book published in 1961.

Joseph[20] also deals with theoretical aspects of the perceptron, as do Block *et al.*[21]. Hay *et al.*[22] discuss practical perceptron design and give photographs, while Bushor[23] also gives a general description and a photograph of an association unit. Brain[24] suggested the use of multi-aperture magnetic cores in the perceptron as neural elements. In a theoretical study, Keller[25] pointed out the importance of time delays in perceptron systems. Daly *et al.*[26] suggested theoretical improvements in perceptron-type systems, while Chichinadze[27] again considered the theory of perceptrons. Work on perceptrons seems to have been very well supported in the United States. While it is clearly hoped that there will eventually be some useful results, the work published in the past decade has been somewhat erudite.

Grimsdale *et al.*[28] divided the visible field into 64 lines each of 40 elements. A computer was then programmed to divide the pattern being scanned into meaningful segments by discarding information which appeared to be doubtful, e.g. that due to a spot of dirt on the paper. A definite subdividing routine was then followed to form the pattern into segments. Using a medium-speed computer, an averaging time of about 60 sec was required to recognise each character. It is significant that it was found possible to recognise patterns, once the 'teaching' phase was completed, regardless of their angular orientation. It was pointed out that several completely different patterns could represent the same character, for example A and a. Consequently, they differentiate pattern recognition from character recognition. Grimsdale and Bullingham[29] describe further work and consider briefly the possibility of incorporating an automatic learning procedure into this system.

Taylor[30] suggested that it is more economical to use a television camera and a synchronous gate rather than a matrix of photocells for visual pattern recognition. He also later discussed the use of a mechanical switch scanner, combined with a capacitor bank for short-term memory. He stresses the advantage of analogue machines over digital machines in the generalisation process, or where parts of a pattern are missing. However, Tizard, in the discussion, feels that this point is overstressed and that it is not a fundamental

factor. Taylor pointed out that the earlier pattern recognition systems were unduly sensitive to intensity, so that patterns with insufficient contrast could not be recognised. He based his own system on the use of the artificial neurons which he had described in 1956. These give an output signal only when the sum of the input signals exceeds a certain positive value, in other words a threshold logic arrangement is involved.

Taylor suggests that the details of the patterns to be recognised should be more finely subdivided at the centre of the field of vision than at the outside, rather than uniformly divided into squares. One would suggest here that this could be achieved automatically by subdivision of the visual field by concentric circles and radial lines, rather than into squares. Taylor shows how to interconnect the basic units so as to detect the largest of several signals, and how to obtain contrast enhancement. He was able to demonstrate a limited amount of pattern discrimination with a reasonably concise assembly

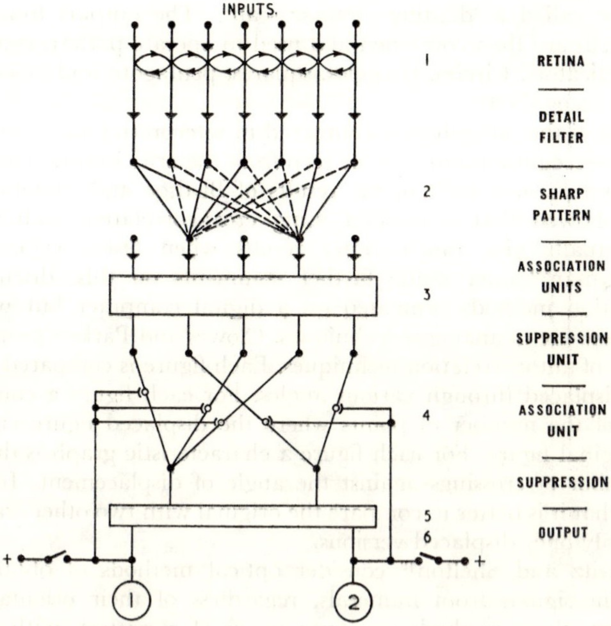

Fig. 7. Taylor's pattern-learning machine

as illustrated in Fig. 7. In 1964, Taylor[31] published details of transistorised sub-units of his form of pattern recogniser.

Bailey[32] has described some commercial work on character-

recognition machines. Sprick and Ganzhorn[33] proposed the splitting of patterns into right-hand and left-hand halves for identification. By this means a characteristic sequence of positive and negative pulses is obtained, regardless of location, size or tilt, though smudges, etc. can cause difficulty. Young[34] discussed this work together with other work including a small machine for recognising numbers as they are handwritten into a special aperture. The problems associated with visual character recognition are then considered, and the simplest possible verbal general description of the capital letter 'A' is derived, as a basis for a character-recognition logic.

In 1960, Roberts[35] described a pattern-recognition programme for a digital computer which achieved a 94% success after a training period of 40 trials, working at the recognition rate of four characters per second. Stearns[36] used arrays of diode elements to achieve 99% success in recognition of clean typewritten characters. Harmon[37] described the circuitry and construction of a machine in which 32 separate photocells were used, each to scan along a radial line in what he called a 'dilating circular scan'. The outputs from the photocells are then combined and used to operate pattern-recognition indicators. Circles, triangles, squares, pentagons and hexagons can be recognised.

Some of the difficulties encountered in interpreting the results of pattern-recognition tests can be seen from the criticism by Highleyman and Kamentsky[38] of the results of Bledsoe and Browning.[39] They showed that a method using cross-correlation techniques can actually give much better results when tested rigorously. Highleyman[40] later made further comments on this, discussing correlation methods simulated on a digital computer but which can make use of analogue techniques. Clowes and Parks[41] proposed the use of autocorrelation techniques. Each figure is compared with itself displaced through various angles. For each figure a count is made of the number of points where the displaced figure crosses the original figure. For each figure a characteristic graph is drawn of number of crossings against the angle of displacement. It was found that it is better to compare the original with two other (rather than only one) displaced versions.

Horwitz and Shelton[42] consider optical methods of obtaining invariant signals from numerals, regardless of their orientation. In effect, these methods use comparison of a pattern with itself when moved through various distances and angles. They consider the theory and give photographs of the two-dimensional autocorrelation functions, obtained by comparing each numeral with displaced versions of itself, which their scheme gives in practice. One point of note from their photographs is the way in which the

shape of our arabic numerals falls into related pairs, 0-5, 1-6, 2-7, 3-8, 4-9, though they do not mention this fact.

The Adaline (or Adaptive Linear) pattern-recognition system described by Widrow and Hoff[43] uses artificial adjustable neurons. An input pattern is divided into 16 (4 x 4) elements, and when any particular pattern is presented the training operator turns a two-way 'reference' switch to + or − depending on the neural response required for this pattern. All inputs to the artificial neuron are then adjusted by an identical amount to reduce the output of the neuron to zero. The 'training' phase proceeds in this manner until, after 50 or so input patterns have been presented, the unit gives the correct outputs as required. Consideration was also given to the use of networks of these devices. Later developments were described by Widrow *et al.*,[44] including applications to speech recognition, electrocardiogram diagnosis and weather forecasting. Duda and Machanik[45] also discuss the use of threshold logic units for weather forecasting. Problems involved in the visual scanning of practical printed characters are discussed by Merry and Norrie.[46]

Minsky[47] reviews the field and discusses systematic methods of symbolic description of complex patterns. He brings out well the tendency of workers in these fields of study to proceed to more complex problems before having mastered simpler ones. Kamentsky[48] described three computer programmes for interpreting whole rows of hand-written numerals, for example telephone numbers written down by an operator handling a call. One of these programmes is due to Dimond.[49] The shape of the written numerals is constrained in different ways for the three programmes. For example, one of the methods uses pre-printed dots to indicate the required writing positions. Freeman[50] described his SCRIPT (Simulator for a Character Recognition Instrument through Programming Technology!) programme for a digital computer, which compares digital patterns, produced by scanning, with previously encountered patterns.

Gamba proposed the PAPA (Probabilistic Automatic Programmer/Analyser) type of pattern-recognition machine which was the subject of a number of short Italian papers in 1961 and 1962. A chessboard pattern (8 x 8) is used for the input and the machine is also used to recognise musical phrases when they are encoded (Gamba *et al.*[51]). The machine produces punched cards for analysis by a digital computer. Borsellino and Gamba[52] outlined the mathematical theory of PAPA and suggested an analogy with quantum mechanics. Palmieri[53] described the circuitry of the first PAPA machine, together with modifications intended to eliminate the external computer. With Sanna, he also described with photo-

graph a new self-contained machine which they called PAPA 2. He also proposed[54] a method of high-speed operation using flying-spot scanners. Gamba *et al.*[55] described a pattern-recognition experiment with PAPA 2.

Alt[56] suggested the use of mathematical 'moments' as pattern descriptions which will not vary with the displacement of the patterns. He programmed a digital computer to carry out his procedure with a 176 x 176 visual matrix. Hu[57] had earlier suggested a similar approach. Doyle[58] proposed spiral scanning of a transparent image and the production of an autocorrelation signal by optical means. Optical autocorrelation had been discussed earlier by Kovasznay and Arman,[59] while Meyer-Eppler and Darius[60] had shown how to construct visual autocorrelograms of shapes by passing light from a uniform source through two transparencies of the same pattern. They give cross-correlograms of the first five letters of the alphabet. Revesz and Shen[61] discussed optical filtering for pre-processing in object recognition as a method of simplifying decision-making networks and reducing noise effects. Doyle[58] obtained good pattern recognition independently of location, orientation and size and in the presence of interfering noise of amplitude equal to, or even stronger than, that of the pattern being detected.

Fischler *et al.*[62, 63] discussed the classification of patterns into three different classes based on eight sub-classes, and they considered the use of threshold (neuron-type) logic elements in the recognition process. They consider pattern recognition as consisting of two basic processes, firstly abstraction of significant features and secondly identification of the particular pattern giving rise to these features. Mattson and Firschein[64] continued this work, using the PIP (Pattern Information Processor) machine. Julesz[65] showed that the recognition of patterns of dots in a noisy background depends on the uniformity of the brightness or the colour of the dots.

Lewis[66] considers which statistical characteristics of letters and alphabets are important in pattern recognition. Using a computer, he obtained about 82% correct recognition from 15 complete 62-symbol alphabets, using a set of 13 basic characteristics for recognition. This was not a learning system, since it could only select characteristics supplied to it by its designer. His sample letters were quantized on a 36 x 36 grid ('by a completely disinterested and bored girl') and scanned, the resulting binary number being examined. Methods of splitting up handwritten letters into standard line sections and so classifying them for recognition were presented by Eden[67].

In 1962, David and Selfridge[68] briefly reviewed the field of pattern recognition. They give a useful comparative table of 10 of

the methods of visual character recognition which have been used. They say that we are a long way indeed from the point where a computer can understand any but the most primitive English. They question the need for a computer which could, for example, read and translate *Isvestia*, since in the end a man must read and understand the result. A very large and complex piece of electronic equipment would be required merely to replace one human tedium with another.

Highleyman[69] follows Chow[70] in considering decision functions for pattern recognition. He limits his discussion to linear functions approximating to the desired functions because the former are more easily mechanised. Consequently, he imagines all the characteristics of any pattern to be plotted in a multidimensional space which is divided up by planes. In order to classify any point of the pattern, it is then only necessary to decide on which side of each plane the point in question lies. He points out that his derived equation in fact describes an artificial neuron, a perceptron or an Adaline, and it is easily mechanised. He used a 12 x 12 matrix to obtain a 144-bit description of handwritten numerals, though the results were disappointing. However, Highleyman claimed that this method would perform at least as well as some other systems. Braverman[71] described a similar process, his 'compactness' algorism giving good results using a 6 x 10 matrix. A total of 796 written numerals were used, 202 of them in the learning process and the rest in testing. Results of over 90% successful recognition were obtained. Griffin *et al.*[72] combined the 'linear decision function' hyperspace division technique of Highleyman, using resistor inputs to linear amplifiers, with the perceptron.

Brailovskii[73] describes a computer programme based on 'conditional entropy' for learning pattern recognition. It was found useful in the design and interpretation of biological experiments. Ullman[74] applied the 'Lernmatrix' of Steinbuch[75] to pattern recognition. He simulated it on a computer and set it to learn to recognise patterns of six digits. Bonner[76] described a programme for designing a pattern-recognition system which operates by splitting complex patterns into more elementary parts. Freeman[77] discusses a method of classification of line patterns which can be used for pattern recognition.

Hu[78] points out that pattern recognition based on a check-list of properties cannot easily handle patterns not previously encountered. Statistical methods, on the other hand, can easily handle new patterns, but they cannot be made independent of size, position and orientation. Hu presents a method of obtaining independence of orientation using the mathematical technique of

moment invariants. He uses a 16 x 16 matrix and computes values of 'spread' and of 'slenderness' for each pattern to be recognised. It was clear that these two parameters alone would be insufficient to differentiate all letters of the alphabet reliably, even when drawn using stencils.

Kamentsky and Liu[79] use a flying-spot scanner to reduce optical images of typed characters to magnetic tape-recordings of a pattern of 1's and 0's. The information is then fed into a computer which is programmed to examine the results which are obtainable with many different possible logical pattern recognition circuits, to select the best circuit arrangement and to test it. The computer produces the specifications of circuits consisting of 39 to 96 logical 'AND' gates connected to a computer shift register and to a resistor network comparison system. In this way they convert the recognition of light and dark spaces into the recognition of time patterns of pulses. They obtained recognition errors of less than 1%.

Greanias *et al.*[80] use a flying-spot scanner which first scans in a series of small circular patterns along straight lines over any pattern to be recognised. When the scanning spot encounters a line, it follows the line right around the figure described by the line. The resulting information about the shape of the figure is passed on after smoothing out the circular motion. The diameter of the circular motion is automatically adjusted after the first scanning in order to compensate for the size of the pattern, which is restricted within a 2 in. × 3 in. area. Various key features of the pattern are then noted and used in the recognition logical circuits. Altogether 800 transistors are required for the logic and 200 for the line direction and location signals, with 400 transistors in the beam control circuits.

Akers *et al.*[81] mention the many different names which have been used for majority-logic units, and they describe a method of using these for pattern recognition, to supplement existing techniques. Low[82] discussed the various forms of neuron which have been produced and then considered the problems caused by drifts of operating points encountered with the ADALINE pattern-recognition system. Low's Defective Adaline (DADALINE) computer programme allowed simulated defects to be introduced. He found that none of the defects encountered in artificial neurons (variable gain elements) has a significant effect on system stability or on system generalisation, though some defects could increase the required learning time by up to two times.

Widrow *et al.*[83] describe a manually-operated version of the ADALINE (Adaptive Linear Neuron) threshold element, which they call 'Knobby Adaline'. In this there are 16 inputs, arranged

in a 4 x 4 matrix, together with an adjustable threshold level control. There is also an adjustable control in each of the 16 input circuits. When any input pattern is presented, the controls are adjusted, in accordance with a defined procedure, until the unit gives the required output. Another input pattern is then presented. Experimentally, about 50 attempts are required before the unit can be regarded as fully trained to differentiate successfully between three different input patterns T, G and F.

Brain *et al.*[84] describe the learning machine MINOS 2. This uses 66 threshold logic elements connected in a similar way to the Madaline device. A total of 100 planoconvex lenses are used in an optical pre-processor. The lenses focus images of the pattern to be recognised on to the plane of a prepared optical mask which takes the place of input resistors to the threshold logic units. Each logic unit merely comprises a photocell, an amplifier and a four-layer semiconductor diode. Unfortunately, their description of the rest of the machine is not very clear, though block diagrams of the system are given. Magnetic cores are used, following the Crafts second-harmonic scheme, in the memory and control sections of MINOS 2. No results are given.

Levin and Sapozhnikov[85] considered the coding of hand-drawn patterns based on the intersections of the patterns with eight radii of an enclosing circle. Lowitz[86] introduces an approach to a theoretical method of pattern recognition based on the production of a spectral form of a pattern. Aizerman[87] discusses algorithms which can be used to divide up patterns for classification. Good results were obtained when the procedures were programmed on to a digital computer. The nature of the strokes making up handwriting was considered by Mermelstein and Eden,[88] who also discussed the use of this information in a computer to recognise handwritten symbols. Greenberg and Konheim[89] investigated computer programmes for pattern-recognition algorithms. Cooper[90] has described methods of optical signal processing.

REFERENCES

1. YOUNG, J. F., 'Cybernetics, Past, Present and Future', *Brit. Comm. Electron.*, **12**, 302 (1965)
2. FLOWER, J. B., 'A Typewriter that Copies with Its Own Eye', *Sci. Amer.*, **114**, 323 (1916); *see also* 'True Nature of Speech', *Proc. A.I.E.E.*, **35**, 183 (1916)
3. GLOVAZKY, A., 'Determination of Redundancies in a Set of Patterns', *Trans. I.R.E.*, **IT2**, 151 (1956)
4. RIEKEMAN, E. C., *et al.*, 'Determination of Redundancies in a Set of Patterns', *Trans. I.R.E.*, **IT3**, 167 (1957)
5. GILL, A., 'Minimum-Scan Pattern-Recognition', *Trans. I.R.E.*, **IT5**, 52 (1959)
6. GREANIAS, E. C., *et al.*, 'The Design of Logic for the Recognition of Printed Characters by Simulation', *I.B.M.J.*, **1**, 8 (1957)

7. TAYLOR, W. K., 'Visual Organisation', *Nature*, **182**, 29 (1958)
8. MACKAY, D. M., 'Moving Visual Images Produced by Regular Stationary Patterns', *Nature*, **180**, 849 (1957)
9. LETTVIN, J. Y., *et al.*, 'What the Frog's Eye Tells the Frog's Brain', *Proc. I.R.E.*, **47**, 1940 (1959)
10. HARTLINE, H. K., 'The Modification of Sensory Information by Neural Interaction in the Eye, and its Relation to Vision', *Trans. I.R.E.*, **ME6**, 84 (1959)
11. RIGGS, L. A., *et al.*, 'The Disappearance of Steadily Fixated Visual Test Objects', *J.O.S.A.*, **43**, 495 (1953)
12. KAPANY, N. S., 'Fiber Optics', *Scient. Amer.*, **203**, 72 (1960)
13. UNGER, S. H., 'Pattern Detection and Recognition', *Proc I.R.E.*, **47**, 1737 (1959)
14. UNGER, S. H., 'A Computer Oriented Toward Spatial Problems', *Proc I.R.E.*, **46**, 1744 (1958)
15. GREENE, P. H., 'Networks for Pattern Perception,' *Proc N.E.C.*, **15**, 357 (1959); *see also*, 'An Approach to Computers that Learn', *W.J.C.C.*, **15**, 181 (1959)
16. ROSENBLATT, F., 'The Perceptron, A Probabilistic Model for Information Storage and Organisation in the Brain', *Psych. Rev.*, **65**, 386 (1958)
17. ROSENBLATT, F., 'Two Theorems of Statistical Separability in the Perceptron', *Mechanisation of Thought Processes*, **1**, 513, H.M.S.O. (1959)
18. ROSENBLATT, F., 'Perceptron Simulation Experiments', *Proc. I.R.E.*, **48**, 301 (1960)
19. MURRAY, A. E., 'A Review of the Perceptron Program', *Proc. N.E.C.*, **15**, 346 (1959); *see also* ROSENBLATT, F., *Principles of Neurodynamics*, Spartan (1961)
20. JOSEPH, R. D., 'On Predicting Perceptron Performance', *I.R.E. Internat. Conv. Record*, **8**, (2), 71 (1960)
21. BLOCK, H. D., *et al.*, 'Analysis of a Four-Layer, Series-Coupled Perceptron', *Rev. Mod. Phys.*, **34**, 135 (1962)
22. HAY, J. C., *et al.*, 'The Mark I Perceptron—Design and Performance', *I.R.E. Internat. Conv. Record*, **8**, (2), 78 (1960)
23. BUSHOR, W. E., 'The Perceptron; An Experiment in Learning', *Electronics*, **33**, 56 (1960)
24. BRAIN, A. E., 'The Simulation of Neural Elements by Electrical Networks Based on Multi-Aperture Magnetic Cores', *Proc. I.R.E.*, **49**, 49 (1961)
25. KELLER, H. B., 'Finite Automata, Pattern Recognition and Perceptrons', *J.A.C.M.*, **8**, 1 (1961)
26. DALY, J. A., *et al.*, 'An Iterative Design Technique for Pattern Classification Logic', *I.E.E.E. Wescon*, Pt. 4, (1963)
27. CHICHINADZE, V. K., 'On the Dynamics of Some Learning and Self-Learning Processes', *Autom. Remote Contr.*, 453 (1964)
28. GRIMSDALE, R. L., *et al.*, 'A System for the Automatic Recognition of Patterns', *Proc. I.E.E.*, **106B**, 210 (1959)
29. GRIMSDALE, R. L., and BULLINGHAM, J. M., 'Character Recognition by Digital Computer Using a Special Flying-Spot Scanner', *Comp. J.*, **4**, 129 (1961)
30. TAYLOR, W. K., 'Automatic Control by Visual Signals', *Mechanisation of Thought Processes*, **2**, 849, 951, H.M.S.O. (1959)
31. TAYLOR, W. K., 'A Pattern-Recognising Adaptive Controller', *Autom. Remote Contr.*, 488 (1964)
32. BAILEY, C. E. G., 'Automatic Reading of Typed or Printed Characters', *J. Brit. I.R.E.*, **17**, 138 (1957)
33. SPRICK, W., and GANZHORN, K., 'Recognition of Numbers by Contour Following', *Proc. I.E.E.*, **106B**, 448 (1959)
34. YOUNG, D. A., 'Automatic Character Recognition', *Electron. Eng.*, **32**, 2 (1960)
35. ROBERTS, L. G., 'Pattern Recognition with an Adaptive Network', *I.R.E. Conv. Rec.*, **8**, (2), 66 (1960)

36. STEARNS, S. D., 'A Method for the Design of Pattern-Recognition Logic', *Trans. I.R.E.*, **EC9**, 48 (1960)
37. HARMON, L. D., 'Line-Drawing Pattern-Recogniser', *Electronics*, **33**, 39 (1960)
38. HIGHLEYMAN, W. H., and KAMENTSKY, L. A., 'Comments on a Character-Recognition Method of Bledsoe and Browning', *Trans. I.R.E.*, **EC9**, 263 (1960)
39. BLEDSOE, W. W., and BROWNING, I., 'Pattern Recognition and Reading By Machine', *E.J.C.C.*, **16**, 225, 233 (1959)
40. HIGHLEYMAN, W. H., 'A Note on Optimum Pattern Recognition Systems', *Trans. I.R.E.*, **EC10**, 97, 287, 502 (1961)
41. CLOWES, M. B., and PARKS, J. R., 'A New Technique in Automatic Character Recognition', *Computer J.*, **4**, 121 (1961)
42. HORWITZ, L. P., and SHELTON, G. L., 'Pattern Recognition Using Auto-Correlation', *Proc. I.R.E.*, **49**, 175 (1961)
43. WIDROW, B., and HOFF, M. E., 'Adaptive Switching Circuits', *I.R.E. Wescon*, **4**, (4), 96 (1960)
44. WIDROW, B., *et al.*, 'Practical Applications for Adaptive Data-Processing Systems', *I.E.E.E. Wescon*, Pt. 7, Paper 11.4 (1963)
45. DUDA, R. O., and MACHANIK, J. W., 'An Adaptive Prediction Technique and its Application to Weather Forecasting', *I.E.E.E. Wescon*, Pt. 7, Paper 11.3 (1963)
46. MERRY, I. W., and NORRIE, G. O., 'Character Quality and Scanner Organisation', *Comp. J.*, **4**, 137 (1961)
47. MINSKY, M., 'Steps Towards Artificial Intelligence', *Proc. I.R.E.*, **49**, 8 (1961)
48. KAMENTSKY, L. A., 'Simulation of Three Machines which Read Rows of Numbers', *Trans. I.R.E.*, **EC10**, 489 (1961)
49. DIMOND, T. L., 'Devices for Reading Handwritten Characters', *E.J.C.C.*, **12**, 232 (1957)
50. FREEMAN, D. N., 'Computer Synthesis of Character Recognition Systems', *Trans. I.R.E.*, **EC10**, 735 (1961)
51. GAMBA, A., 'Optimum Performance of Learning Machines', *Proc. I.R.E.*, **49**, 348 (1961)
52. BORSELLINO, A., and GAMBA, A., 'An Outline of a Mathematical Theory of PAPA', *Supp. Nuovo Cimento*, **20**, 221 (1961)
53. PALMIERI, G., and SANNA, R., 'A New PAPA Machine', *Supp. Nuovo Cimento*, **23**, 266 (1962)
54. PALMIERI, G., 'A Proposal for a High Speed PAPA', *Supp. Nuovo Cimento*, **23**, 276 (1962)
55. GAMBA, A., *et al.*, 'Preliminary Experimental Results with PAPA No. 2', *Supp. Nuovo Cimento*, **23**, 280 (1962)
56. ALT, F. L., 'Digital Pattern Recognition by Moments', *J.A.C.M.*, **9**, 240 (1962)
57. HU, M. K., 'Pattern Recognition by Moment Invariants', *Proc. I.R.E.*, **49**, 1428 (1961)
58. DOYLE, W., 'Operations Useful for Similarity Invariant Pattern Recognition', *J.A.C.M.*, **9**, 259 (1962)
59. KOVASZNAY, L. S. G., and ARMAN, A., 'Optical Auto-Correlation Measurement of Two-Dimensional Random Patterns', *Rev. Sci. Inst.*, **28**, 793 (1957)
60. MEYER-EPPLER, W., and DARIUS, G., 'Two-Dimensional Photographic Auto-correlation of Pictures and Alphabet Letters', *Information Theory* (Ed. C. Cherry), Butterworths, 34 (1956)
61. REVESZ, G., and SHEN, D. W. C., 'The Application of Electro-Optical Filtering to Object Recognition', *I.E.E.E. Conv. Record*, **12**, (1), 130 (1964)
62. FISCHLER, M., *et al.*, 'An Approach to General Pattern Recognition', *Trans. I.R.E.*, **IT8**, S64 (1962)
63. FISCHLER, M. A., 'On The Statistical Independence of Features in a Switching Theory Model for Pattern Recognition', *Proc. I.E.E.E.*, **51**, 1370 (1963)

64. MATTSON, R. L., and FIRSCHEIN, O., 'Feature Word Construction for use with Pattern Recognition Algorithms, An Experimental Study', *A.C.M.J.*, **10**, 458 (1963)
65. JULESZ, B., 'Visual Pattern Discrimination', *Trans. I.R.E.*, **IT8**, 179 (1962)
66. LEWIS, P. M., 'The Characteristic Selection Problem in Recognition Systems', *Trans. I.R.E.*, **IT8**, 172 (1962)
67. EDEN, M., 'Handwriting and Pattern Recognition', *Trans. I.R.E.*, **IT8**, 160 (1962)
68. DAVID, E. E., and SELFRIDGE, O. G., 'Eyes and Ears for Computers', *Proc. I.R.E.*, **50**, 1093 (1962)
69. HIGHLEYMAN, W. H., 'Linear Decision Functions With Application to Pattern Recognition', *Proc. I.R.E.*, **50**, 1501 (1962)
70. CHOW, C. K., 'An Optimum Character Recognition System Using Decision Functions', *Trans. I.R.E.*, **EC6**, 247 (1957)
71. BRAVERMAN, E. M., 'Experiments in Teaching a Machine to Recognise Visual Patterns', *Autom. Remote Contr.*, **23**, 315 (1962)
72. GRIFFIN, J. S., KING, J. H., and TUNIS, C. J., 'Pattern Identification Using Adaptive Linear Decision Functions', *I.E.E.E. Wescon*, Paper 6.4 (1963)
73. BRAILOVSKII, V. L., 'A Method for the Recognition of Objects Described by Several Parameters, With Some Possible Applications', *Autom. Remote Contr.*, **23**, 1542 (1962)
74. ULLMAN, J. R., 'A Consistency Technique for Pattern Association', *Trans. I.R.E.*, **IT8**, S74 (1962)
75. STEINBUCH, K., 'Die Lernmatrix', *Kybernetik*, **1**, 36 (1961)
76. BONNER, R. E., 'A Logical Pattern-Recognition Program', *I.B.M.J.*, **6**, 353 (1962)
77. FREEMAN, H., 'On the Digital Computer Classification of Geometric Line-Patterns', *Proc. N.E.C.*, **18**, 312 (1962)
78. HU, M. K., 'Visual Pattern Recognition by Moment Invariants', *Trans. I.R.E.*, **IT8**, 179 (1962)
79. KAMENTSKY, L. A., and LIU, C. N., 'Computer-Automated Design of Multi-Fount Print Recognition Logic', *I.B.M.J.*, **7**, 2 (1963)
80. GREANIAS, E. C., *et al.*, 'The Recognition of Handwritten Numerals by Contour Analysis', *I.B.M.J.*, **7**, 14 (1963)
81. AKERS, S. B., and RUTTER, B. H., 'The Use of Threshold Logic in Pattern Recognition', *I.E.E.E. Wescon*, Pt. 4, Paper 1.2 (1963)
82. LOW, P. R., 'Influence of Component Imperfections on Performance of Trainable Systems', *I.E.E.E. Wescon*, Pt. 4, Paper 6.3 (1963)
83. WIDROW, B., *et al.*, 'Practical Applications for Adaptive Data-Processing Systems', *I.E.E.E. Wescon*, Pt. 7, Paper 11.4 (1963)
84. BRAIN, A. E., *et al.*, 'A Large Self-Contained Learning Machine', *I.E.E.E. Wescon*, Pt. 4, Paper 6.1 (1963)
85. LEVIN, I. Y., and SAPOZHNIKOV, L. B., 'Recognition Algorithms', *Autom. Remote Contr.*, **24**, 704 (1963)
86. LOWITZ, G. E., 'Pattern Recognition Method Based on the Linear Separability of the Signal Space', *I.E.E.E. Wescon*, Pt. 4, Paper 1.4 (1963)
87. AIZERMAN, M. A., 'Learning Systems in the Light of Experiments on Teaching the Systems Pattern Recognition', *Autom. Remote Contr.*, **25**, 503 (1964)
88. MERMELSTEIN, P., and EDEN, M., 'Experiments on Computer Recognition of Connected Handwritten Words', *Inf. Contr.*, **7**, 255 (1964)
89. GREENBERG, H. J., and KONHEIM, A. G., 'Linear and Non-Linear Methods in Pattern Classification', *I.B.M.J.*, **8**, 299 (1964)
90. COOPER, D. C., 'Signal Processing Using Optical Techniques', *J.I.E.R.E.*, **32**, 5 (1966)

13

Speech Recognition

It has long been a dream of man that he might produce machines which would recognise and obey his spoken word. In ancient fantasy, the door swung back at the words 'Open Sesame'. Later work was sometimes more practical. Von Kempelen, who is chiefly remembered for the trick chess-player exhibited by Maelzel, nevertheless did some important early work on the analysis of the nature of speech, in an attempt to construct speaking machines. A recent review of this work is that of Dudley and Tarnoczy[1]. Quite recently, Orwell was careful (in *1984*) not to describe too closely the fictional 'speakwrite' which was perhaps a phonetically-operated typewriter. Some have done more than think. Paget[2] constructed a simple toy dog, 'Radio Rex', which would answer to its name. The dog, made of celluloid, had an iron base retained against a spring by an electromagnet. The dog was released by the energy at a frequency of 500 Hz contained in the sound of the spoken name 'Rex', which was used to interrupt the magnet current. However, in order to progress beyond the construction of toys, extensive study of the nature of speech has been necessary. There has been great interest in the analysis and synthesis of speech for communication purposes, and this has led quite naturally to interest in the recognition of words and commands by analysis.

Flower[3] described a voice-operated writing machine in which a number of resonators was used to determine the frequencies present in speech. At the New York World Fair of 1939, a synthetic speaking machine known as the Voder (Voice-Operated Demonstrator) was shown. It is described by Dudley *et al.*,[4] who also review earlier devices. The sounds produced by the Voder were controlled by a trained keyboard operator. The Voder was actually derived from an earlier device, the Vocoder, described by Dudley in 1939.[5-7] An excellent account of the Vocoder was given by Halsey and

Swaffield[8] in 1948, and more recently Swaffield[9] has described later work. The action of the Vocoder is based on the analysis of speech into a number of frequency bands. The acoustic energy contained in each band is then measured. It is found that variations of these energy levels are quite slow, so that they can be transmitted efficiently over a telegraph circuit which would not respond rapidly enough to carry the original speech signals. At the receiving end, the energy-content signals are used to control generators and filters which have the same overall effect as the vocal cords and mouth of a human. In this way, the sound of the original speech is reconstituted or synthesised at the receiving end.

Many of the difficulties obtained with the Vocoder are the psychological ones of the user, who appears to feel that he is being cheated if he knows that he is not hearing the original speech. This problem is artificial, because any telephone link introduces some distortion and the 'original' speech is never heard. Nevertheless, there are some real difficulties of conveying information using the Vocoder, and no doubt these, as well as prejudice, have prevented its commercial use. From the point of view of recognition of speech by a machine, the human psychological problems are absent and the analyser part of a Vocoder forms a promising input arrangement.

Dreyfus-Graf[10] described his 'Steno-sonograph' in which speech is analysed by six frequency-sensitive filters. The outputs of the filters control radial movements of a pen, the radial direction of movement of the pen indicating the frequency content of the speech from 200 to 3,000 Hz. As paper is moved along under the pen, recognisable shapes are drawn which depend on the speech sound being produced. Dreyfus-Graf also proposed a possible Typo-sonograph which, based on a similar action, would type speech sounds. He compares the shapes produced by his machine with Egyptian hieroglyphs or Chinese pictographs. Commenting on this work, Fry and Denes[11] state that the individual voice characteristics of different speakers, the manner and rate of speaking, and the context change the patterns to such an extent that considerable learning would be required in order to be able to read them successfully, even in the most favourable conditions.

One of the problems in work on speech-recognition is the question of how much of the information contained in a speech waveform is really redundant. For example, Licklider and Pollack[12] mention how it had been found that 'clipping' speech waveforms, i.e. preventing them from exceeding a quite small amplitude in either the positive or the negative direction, has a surprisingly small effect on the intelligibility of the speech. It was found best to include a

circuit to differentiate the speech waveform with respect to time, i.e. to introduce a component proportional to the rate of change with time of the signal voltage, before clipping. Carrying out the inverse operation after clipping improved the quality but not the intelligibility of the speech sounds. The differentiation has the effect of boosting the high-frequency content of the speech-voltage waveform. Licklider[13] described further work in 1950. Peterson[14] investigated the possibility of using the knowledge of clipping in speech recognition. Basically, the only information retained after speech clipping is the times at which the speech voltages pass through zero. Chang *et al.*[15] also make use of the instants at which the slope of the speech-voltage waveform is zero in order to obtain additional information about the waveform.

Speech can be divided up into a sequence of elementary units of sound which are known as phonemes. Smith[16] described initial work on a phoneme detector, based on the analysis of speech waveforms into 32 frequency bands and a determination of the speech energy in each band, as in the Vocoder. The difference between the energy signals in each pair of adjacent bands is taken, and then the process is repeated to give the second differences. This is intended to reduce the effects of interfering noise, and it also makes the circuits more selective. For example, if the outputs of three consecutive tuned filters are a, b and c he takes the signal $(b-a) + (b-c) = 2b-a-c$. This gives a sharply selective response and also helps to limit the effects of noise. The signals are infinitely clipped in amplitude before analysis. Babcock[17] has also discussed this method of sharpening the frequency-selectivity of filters.

Davis, Biddulph and Balashek[18,19] described a machine which could automatically recognise spoken digits. The accuracy claimed was 97% to 99% for one individual speaker after adjustment of the machine, though the machine is not suitable for use by any other speaker without readjustment. They divide the speech into two frequency bands, below and above 900 Hz. The number of times that the speech-voltage waveform in each band passes through zero in a given time is then used as a measure of the frequency content in that band. The main frequency of each of the two bands is then compared with prior information stored in memory circuits, to determine the most probable digit being spoken. In effect, they operate by using what are known as the first and second formant frequencies of speech, i.e. the frequencies at which most of the speech energy occurs.

Fry and Denes[11] partially review the field, and they describe the work of Jakobson, Fant and Halle, who found that 15 one-third

octave filters having centre frequencies ranging from 250 Hz to 8 kHz would be the minimum requirements for speech recognition. They operate relays when sound energy occurs simultaneously in pairs of frequency bands, and they also make use of the durations of the coincidences. The speech input is clipped to a low level by removing the peaks. Out of 16 different sounds, 12 could be detected successfully, i.e. incur no more than four or five errors in 150 recognitions.

Lawrence[20] showed that it is possible to synthesise fairly good speech using only four variables, namely three formant frequencies and a driving function. In the discussion on this paper, Carnochan described experiments of Delattre in which a given fixed consonant spectrum was shown to produce apparently different sounds depending on the following vowel. Replying to comments by McKay, Lawrence suggested that the top two formants always follow each other.

Biddulph[21] gave results obtained with the machine described by Bennett[22] of the auto-correlatograms of spoken digits. These are obtained by multiplying the speech waveform by itself delayed by a range of different times, so emphasising any periodic features of the waveform. Bauman *et al.*[23] built a machine including time delays to make it sensitive to the temporal sequence of sounds and so to help with the recognition of long words. Earlier digit recognisers could mistake other sounds for numbers. Von Bekesy[24] drew analogies between the action of the cochlea and the action of the skin of the arm, which can also perceive travelling waves and which displays such features as mutual inhibition of adjacent nerve cells.

Olsen and Belar[25] described a non-learning phonetic typewriter which can type any sentence made up of combinations of the words 'I-can-see-you-type-this-now' or alternatively of 'are-see-a-I-can-you-read-it-so-sir'. An accuracy of 98% was obtained. They described further work in 1962. Marcou and Daguet[26] showed that the information in a speech wave of the mathematical form $a(t)\cos\phi(t)$ is conveyed by the $\cos\phi\ (t)$ factor alone.

Fry and Denes[27] discussed the problem of presenting the output of a speech recogniser in a form suitable for interpretation by a human. The object is presumably to minimise errors caused by the machine, since clearly there is no sense in translating speech into some other form for use by a human who could simply listen to the original speech unless he happens to be deaf. Von Bekesy[28] further discussed the effects of mutual inhibition in skin touch sensations and in hearing in 1957. He also considered the effects of time delays between stimuli, and the apparent spread of stimulation (e.g. of

frequency) with intensity (e.g. loudness). Taylor[29] synthesised intelligible speech from only four sets of frequency-modulated pulses by using a demodulator having a similar transfer characteristic to that of muscle.

Forgie and Hughes[30] describe work using 35 filters to split up speech for use with a digital computer. Forgie *et al.*[31] obtained 98% correct recognition of digits spoken by 10 mixed voices, both male and female. The method is described in more detail by Forgie[32], who makes it clear that information about the duration of vowel sounds must be used if such good recognition is to be obtained. Using duration as a check on recognition using formant-location, the accuracy of recognition was increased from 88% to 93%, using the earlier computer programme. The machine differentiated such words as 'bit', 'bet', 'bot', 'bought', using 35 frequency bandpass filters, each sampled 180 times per second.

Dudley and Balashek[33] briefly review earlier work and then describe their own work on the recognition of spoken digits. They use two analyser-recognisers in tandem. The first splits speech into frequency bands and measures the power in each band, then comparing the measurements with stored information of standard patterns. The second determines the duration patterns of the speech, and by comparison it determines the word being spoken. This machine can successfully recognise digits spoken by one individual or by another person giving a good imitation. It incorporates a 'volume compressor' which limits the range of variation of amplitude of the speech signals and so keeps the amplitude within the operating range of the rest of the equipment. Ten filters are used, and the outputs from these are summated in a manually-set memory matrix of potentiometers followed by a set of amplifiers. Each bandpass filter circuit feeds one column of the matrix, while each amplifier summates the 10 outputs from one row. In this way, 10 different phonetic patterns (such as that due to the sound 'i') each give an output from one of the amplifiers. The outputs from this phonetic-pattern recogniser operate relays which control the word-pattern recogniser. This part of the equipment produces an output corresponding to a particular digit if the durations of the sounds are correct. These durations are quite different for different speakers. Dudley[34] discusses the use of such methods in speech transmission.

David[35] reviewed the field of speech recognition and discussed the number of different phoneme elements of which speech is composed. David *et al.*[36] describe results using a computer to simulate a system in which only the amplitudes and times of occurrence of the maxima and minima (zero slope) portions of a speech wave are transmitted. They stress the advantage of simulation using a

general purpose digital computer compared with simulation using a specially constructed single-purpose machine.

Fry[37] discussed the general problem of speech recognition. He points out that a mechanical speech recogniser must operate using stored statistical data, and he stresses the importance of redundancy in speech. Denes[38] used a set of filters to split the speech spectrum into a number of bands, noting that, in general, each phoneme corresponds to the presence of energy in two of these bands simultaneously. He makes use of this fact to detect phonemes by electronically multiplying together the outputs of pairs of filters, an output from any one electronic multiplier then indicating the presence of a particular phoneme. For example, 'i' is indicated by output from the 250 Hz and 3,200 Hz filters, while 's' is indicated by output from the 6,000 Hz and 8,000 Hz filters. Electronic circuits then select the largest product and thus indicate the probable phoneme. The sound 't' is differentiated from 's' by its duration, and similar methods are used for some other consonants. The information about each phoneme is retained while the next phoneme is being received, since it is necessary to refer to stored information about probable successive pairs of phonemes or 'digrams'. The output from the device is used to operate a typewriter. Using only one speaker, a typing accuracy of 70% was obtained. Denes and Mathews[39] described their experience using a digital computer to simulate a speech-recognition system.

Fry and Denes[40] point out that a given frequency spectrum can convey one phoneme or another depending on context, i.e. there is ambiguity. Gabor[41] says that we can guess from the work of Walter Lawrence that speech-sound perception is six-dimensional. The six parameters which must be controlled to synthesise very human-sounding speech are larynx frequency and intensity, hiss and three formant frequencies.

Fatehchand[42] thoroughly reviewed the problems involved in the field of speech recognition. He states that there is reason to believe that a machine would require a greater data rate (in binary digits per second) than a human in order to recognise speech, though he does not elaborate on this statement. He points out the difficulties of dealing with continuous speech as opposed to separated individual words. The information which must be stored in a speech recogniser he calculates as follows: 732 different common words comprise 75% of those which occur in normal speech. A channel capacity of about 1,000 bits per second is required for band-compression telephony, corresponding to 250 bits per word at 4 words per second. Hence for 732 words, the minimum information to be stored is 732 x 250 = 183,000 binary digits. This must be increased by 30 times if band-

compression is not used, and by a further 10 times to include nearly all of the words in common use. Fatehchand deals thoroughly with the problems involved and he discusses a few of the non-learning speech-recognition machines which have been constructed. He states that no machine exists which can deal with continuous speech, and Lindgren[43] has reaffirmed this, adding that it is unlikely that there will be one before the 1970's.

In 1960 and 1961, Gabor, Wilby and Woodcock [44, 45] described a learning machine intended to predict the future shape of a waveform applied to it. Unfortunately, the idea of the applications of the machine is kept so vague and general that it is difficult to fit it into the general pattern of cybernetic progress. The machine takes 18 past samples of an undefined input and produces an output function containing 94 free variables. The variable coefficients are adjusted automatically, following a suitable strategy, to make the output approach a predetermined target function as closely as possible. Crabbe[46] makes the point that when listening to a broad Scots accent or to a faint telephone call, we have to absorb whole sentences before meaning can become apparent. By taking into account the probable order of phonemes, it is possible to improve recognition machines. Stevens[47] discussed his proposed speech-recognition machine using 36 channels, each sampled 120 times per second.

Putzrath and Martin[48] proposed the use of artificial neurons for speech recognition. Martin[49] also proposed the use of an electrical circuit for simulation of the cochlea. Marill[50] reviewed the field of speech-recognition machines. Kanal *et al.*[51] give the theoretical background to their approach to pattern and speech recognition. They make the point that 100% recognition of design samples does not necessarily imply good performance on unknowns. Their theoretical approach is based on the use of statistical methods, and they report their preliminary practical results on vowel recognition.

Sebestyen[52] approaches the problem from a different point of view, namely recognition of the speaker rather than recognition of the words spoken. Good results were obtained using a digital computer to differentiate between different speakers by comparison of first and second formant frequencies. Unfortunately, other similar purely scientific work has been abused by certain commercial interests who have seriously suggested the use of 'voice-prints' for identification purposes in courts of law. However, a good mimic can give a frequency spectrum almost identical and indistinguishable from that of the person being imitated. Kiang *et al.*[53] describe investigations into the response of the cochlea of the cat to

repetitive clicks. Shoup[54] suggested a suitable approach to the selection of words for testing speech-recognition machines. Halle and Stevens[55] proposed the use of feedback techniques in speech recognition. The idea was that the machine should synthesise speech from its output and compare the synthesised speech with the input speech.

David and Selfridge[56] review the field of voice recognition, pointing out the difficulties faced. They give a useful comparative table of 13 different speech-recognition machines which have been described in the literature. They suggest that $20,000 would be a reasonable selling price for a speech recogniser, since it could replace 5 people if it was used 24 hours a day. Sholtz and Bakis[57] simulated a set of filters on a computer using the approach described by Welch.[58] They then followed definite procedures to recognise digits spoken by 40 different speakers and obtained 96% success. They claim that their procedure is more tolerant of speaker individualities and of sex differences than are some others. Olson *et al.*[59] demonstrated a system which achieves a 98% accuracy when typing from the spoken word. The amplitude of the input signal is first controlled to within given limits and the signal is then applied to eight filters. The outputs of the filters operate relays and, in addition, the outputs of adjacent filters are compared to obtain the first and second derivatives of the input amplitude-frequency curve with respect to frequency by taking differences. The output is compensated for speed of talking by making use of changes in the form of the input to switch to the next recognition step. There are five time steps and an eight binary-digit frequency spectrum, so each word is coded as a binary number of 40 digits. This binary number is compared with numbers remembered in the memory store of the machine. Such numbers are decoded and used to operate a typewriter. The machine can be operated by either English or French speech and it can translate them into English, French or Spanish spoken words or to English, French, German or Spanish typed words. The accuracy obtained was 98% when 200 voicings of a word were used to establish the code.

Stewart[60] bases a suggested block form of pattern-recognition hearing system on known psychological data. Babcock[61] discusses a method of sharpening the response of frequency-sensitive filters by combining the outputs of adjacent filters. Widrow *et al.*[62] described the use of the Adaline system for real-time speech recognition. Speech signals are passed to eight bandpass filters and integrators and used to form a 240 binary-digit pattern for each spoken word. This system, using Adaline networks, can identify words from an 18-word vocabulary with better than 95% reliability after training with

only eight samples per vocabulary word. The system was simulated on a digital computer.

Keidel[63] reviewed knowledge about the animal auditory system, including the question of mutual inhibition demonstrated by Bekesy.[64] Caldwell[65] discussed the recognition of sounds by use of patterns of excitation in the cochlea, and Sackschewsky and Oestreicher further discussed the background to this work. Martin and Talavage[66] described their experimental approach to speech analysis, involving the use of mutual inhibition for contrast enhancement. Stewart discussed the operation of animal acoustic sensory systems in several papers[60, 67, 68] in 1963. Suzuki and Oizumi[69] used an 8-channel Vocoder with a computer for the recognition of vowel sounds. They found that the vowel sound 'u' was the most difficult, since it produces a wide frequency-spread of energy. In 1964 they again discussed the problem of discrimination of vowels from other spoken matter.[70]

Hillix[71] describes a different approach to speech recognition. In effect he uses a simple photocell to produce a form of 'lip-reading'. When he added a signal dependent on air velocity, he was able to obtain reasonably good recognition of spoken digits, even though the tongue was not visible. Maezono[72] notes that the frequency of the fundamental pitch-signal of speech is between 80 Hz and 400 Hz, while the frequency response of a telephone circuit, or of a Vocoder, is 300 Hz to 3,400 Hz. He discusses the design of equipment to extract the fundamental pitch, based on the statistics of speech and on autocorrelation. Sakai and Doshita[73, 74] discuss their approach to speech recognition, based on the separation of vowels and consonants. Kato *et al.*[75] describe their digit recogniser which gives accuracies of about 98% with 20 different male speakers. Their machine samples the speech at the start and end of the voiced part of spoken digits and also 100 millisec after the start.

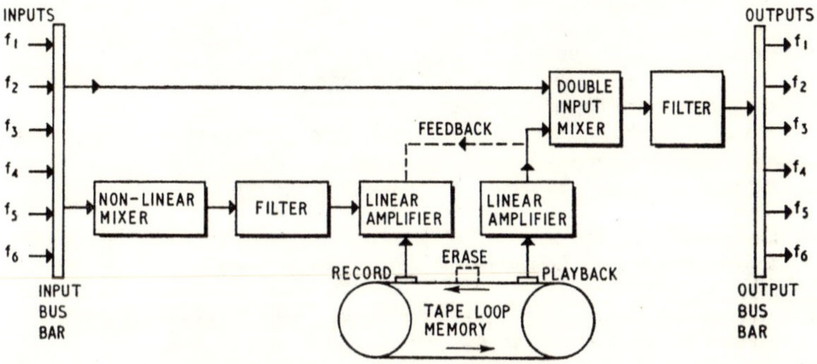

Fig. 8. The writer's early associating machine

The writer's own early (1951) proposal for an associating machine is shown in Fig. 8. High-frequency inputs (e.g. f_1 and f_2) are applied to a mixer and the resulting intermodulation products (e.g. $f_1 - f_2$) are filtered out and recorded. The recording can later be mixed with a future input (e.g. f_2) to produce the associated output (e.g. $f_1 - f_2 + f_2 = f_1$). Unfortunately, practical problems such as non-linearity in the recording system prevent the effective utilisation of such a machine, but more recent work,[76] supported by the Science Research Council, has overcome the problems.

REFERENCES

1. DUDLEY, H., and TARNOCZY, T. H., 'The Speaking Machine of Wolfgang von Kempelen', *J.A.S.A.*, **22**, 151 (1951)
2. PAGET, R., *Human Speech*, Harcourt Brace, 79 (1930)
3. FLOWER, J. B., 'A Typewriter that Copies with its Own Eye', *Sc. Amer.*, **114**, 323 (1916); also 'True Nature of Speech', *Proc. A.I.E.E.*, **35**, 183 (1916)
4. DUDLEY, H., *et al.*, 'A Synthetic Speaker', *J.F.I.*, **227**, 739 (1939)
5. DUDLEY, H., 'Automatic Synthesis of Speech', *Proc. N.A.S.*, **25**, 377 (1939)
6. DUDLEY, H., 'Remaking Speech', *J.A.S.A.*, **11**, 169 (1939)
7. DUDLEY, H., 'The Carrier Nature of Speech', *B.S.T.J.*, **19**, 495 (1940)
8. HALSEY, R. J., and SWAFFIELD, J., 'Analysis-Synthesis Telephony with Special Reference to the Vocoder', *J.I.E.E.*, **95** (3), 391 (1948)
9. SWAFFIELD, J., 'Speech Compression, Electronics and Power', *J.I.E.E.*, **11**, 172 (1965)
10. DREYFUS-GRAF, J., 'Sonograph and Sound Mechanics', *J.A.S.A.*, **22**, 731 (1950)
11. FRY, D. B., and DENES, P., 'Mechanical Speech Recognition', *Communication Theory* (Ed. W. Jackson), Butterworths, 426 (1953)
12. LICKLIDER, J. C. R., and POLLACK, J., 'Effects of Differentiation, Integration and Infinite Peak Clipping Upon the Intelligibility of Speech', *J.A.S.A.*, **20**, 42 (1948)
13. LICKLIDER, J. C. R., 'The Intelligibility of Amplitude-Dichotomised Time-Quantised Speech Waves', *J.A.S.A.*, **22**, 820 (1950)
14. PETERSON, E., 'Frequency Detection and Speech Formants', *J.A.S.A.*, **23**, 668 (1951)
15. CHANG, S. H., *et al.*, 'Representation of Speech Sounds and Some of Their Statistical Properties', *Proc. I.R.E.*, **39**, 147 (1951); *see also* 'The Intervalgram as a Visual Representation of Speech Sounds', *J.A.S.A.*, **23**, 675 (1951)
16. SMITH, C. P., 'A Phoneme Detector', *J.A.S.A.*, **23**, 446 (1951)
17. BABCOCK, M. L., 'Some Uses and Misuses of Bio-Computer Philosophy', *I.E.E.E. Wescon*, Paper 3.1 (1964)
18. DAVIS, K. H., *et al.*, 'Automatic Recognition of Spoken Digits', *J.A.S.A.*, **24**, 637 (1952); *see also J.A.S.A.*, **25**, 832 (1953)
19. DAVIS, K. H., *et al.*, 'Automatic Recognition of Spoken Digits', *Communication Theory* (Ed. W. Jackson), Butterworths, 633 (1953)
20. LAWRENCE, W., 'The Synthesis of Speech Form Signals Which Have a Low Information Rate', *Communication Theory* (Ed. W. Jackson), Butterworths, 460 (1953)
21. BIDDULPH, R., 'Short-Term Auto-Correlation Analysis and Correlatograms of Spoken Digits', *J.A.S.A.*, **26**, 539 (1954)
22. BENNETT, W. R., 'The Correlatograph; A Machine for Continuous Display of Short-Term Correlation', *B.S.T.J.*, **32**, 1173 (1953)

23. BAUMAN, R. H., *et al.*, 'An Electronic Word-Recogniser', *J.A.S.A.*, **26**, 137 (1954)
24. VON BEKESY, G., 'Human Skin Perception of Travelling Waves Similar to Those on the Cochlea', *J.A.S.A.*, **27**, 830 (1955)
25. OLSEN, H. F., and BELAR, H., 'Phonetic Typewriter', *J.A.S.A.*, **28**, 1072 (1956)
26. MARCOU, P., and DAGUET, J., 'A New Method of Speech Transmission', *Ann. Telecomm.*, **11**, 118 (1956)
27. FRY, D. B., and DENES, P., 'On Presenting The Output of a Mechanical Speech-Recogniser', *J.A.S.A.*, **29**, 364 (1957)
28. VON BEKESY, G., 'Sensations on the Skin Similar to Directional Hearing, Beats and Harmonics of the Ear', *J.A.S.A.*, **29**, 489 (1957); *see also* 'Neural Volleys and the Similarity Between Some Sensations Produced by Tones and by Skin Vibrations', *J.A.S.A.*, **29**, 1059 (1957)
29. TAYLOR, W. K., 'The Structure and Functioning of the Nervous System', *Nature*, **180**, 1388 (1957)
30. FORGIE, J. W., and HUGHES, G. W., 'A Real-Time Speech Input System for a Digital Computer' (abstract), *J.A.S.A.*, **30**, 668 (1958)
31. FORGIE, J. W., *et al.*, 'Automatic Recognition of Spoken Digits' (abstract), *J.A.S.A.*, **30**, 669 (1958)
32. FORGIE, J. W., and FORGIE, C. D., 'Results Obtained from a Vowel Recognition Computer Program', *J.A.S.A.*, **31**, 1480 (1959)
33. DUDLEY, H., and BALASHEK, S., 'Automatic Recognition of Phonetic Patterns in Speech', *J.A.S.A.*, **30**, 721 (1958)
34. DUDLEY, H., 'Phonetic Pattern Recognition Vocoder for Narrow-Band Speech Transmission', *J.A.S.A.*, **30**, 733 (1958)
35. DAVID, E. E., 'Artificial Auditory Recognition in Telephony', *I.B.M.J.*, **2**, 294 (1958)
36. DAVID, E. E., *et al.*, 'Description and Results of Experiments with Speech Using Digital Computer Simulation', *I.R.E. Wescon*, **2**, Pt. 7, 3 (1958)
37. FRY, D. B., 'Theoretical Aspects of Mechanical Speech Recognition', *J. Brit. I.R.E.*, **19**, 211 (1959)
38. DENES, P., 'The Design and Operation of the Mechanical Speech Recogniser at University College, London', *J. Brit. I.R.E.*, **19**, 219 (1959)
39. DENES, P., and MATHEWS, M. V., 'Spoken-Digit Recognition Using Time-Frequency Matching', *J.A.S.A.*, **32**, 1450 (1960)
40. FRY, D. B., and DENES, P., 'An Analogue of the Speech Recognition Process', *Mechanisation of Thought Processes*, **1**, 377, H.M.S.O. (1959)
41. GABOR, D., *Trans. I.R.E.*, **IT5**, 97 (1959)
42. FATEHCHAND, R., 'Machine Recognition of Spoken Words', *Advances in Computers*, **1**, 193 (1960)
43. LINDGREN, N., 'Machine Recognition of Human Language', *I.E.E.E. Spectrum*, 45, 114 (1965)
44. GABOR, D., WILBY, W. P. L., and WOODCOCK, R., 'A Self-Optimising Non-Linear Filter, Predictor and Simulator', *Information Theory*, 1960 (Ed. C. Cherry), Butterworths, 348 (1961)
45. GABOR, D., WILBY, W. P. L., and WOODCOCK, R., 'Universal Non-Linear Filter, Predictor and Simulator Which Optimises Itself by a Learning Process', *Proc. I.E.E.*, **108B**, 422 (1961)
46. CRABBE, H. J. F., 'Recognition and Control of Speech', *Automat. Prog.*, 15 (1960)
47. STEVENS, K. N., 'Toward a Model for Speech Recognition', *J.A.S.A.*, **32**, 47 (1960)
48. PUTZRATH, F. L., and MARTIN, T. B., 'Speech Recognition by Neural Networks', *Proc. N.E.C.*, **17**, 311 (1961)
49. MARTIN, T. B., 'Analog Signal Processing by Neural Networks', *Proc. N.E.C.*, **17**, 317 (1961)

50. MARILL, T., 'Automatic Recognition of Speech', *Trans.I.R.E.*, **HFE2**, 2, 34 (1961)
51. KANAL, L., *et al.*, 'Basic Principles of Some Pattern Recognition Systems', *Proc. N.E.C.*, **18**, 279 (1962)
52. SEBESTYEN, G., 'Pattern Recognition by an Adaptive Process of Sample Set Construction', *Trans. I.R.E.*, **IT8, S82** (1962)
53. KIANG, N. Y., *et al.*, 'Temporal Coding of Neural Responses to Acoustic Stimuli', *Trans. I.R.E.*, **IT8**, 113 (1962)
54. SHOUP, J. E., 'Phoneme Selection for Studies in Automatic Speech Recognition', *J.A.S.A.*, **34**, 397 (1962)
55. HALLE, M., and STEVENS, K., 'Speech Recognition; A Model and a Program for Research', *Trans. I.R.E.*, **IT8**, 155 (1962)
56. DAVID, E. E., and SELFRIDGE, O. G., 'Eyes and Ears for Computers', *Proc. I.R.E.*, **50**, 1093 (1962)
57. SHOLTZ, P. N., and BAKIS, R., 'Spoken Digit Recognition Using Vowel-Consonant Segmentation', *J.A.S.A.*, **34**, 1 (1962)
58. WELCH, P. D., 'A Direct Digital Method of Power Spectrum Estimation', *I.B.M.J.*, **5**, 141 (1961)
59. OLSEN, H. F., *et al.*, 'Demonstration of a Speech-Processing System Consisting of a Speech Analyser, Translator, Typer and Synthesiser', *J.A.S.A.*, **34**, 1535 (1962); *see also* 'Print-Out System for the Automatic Recording of the Spectral Analysis of Spoken Syllables', *op. cit.*, 166 (1962)
60. STEWART, J. L., 'Quantitative Laws for Sensory Perception', *Psych. Rev.*, **70**, 180 (1963)
61. BABCOCK, M. L., 'Some Uses and Misuses of Bio-Computer Philosophy', *I.E.E.E. Wescon*, Paper 3.1 (1964)
62. WIDROW, B., *et al.*, 'Practical Applications for Adaptive Data-Processing Systems', *I.E.E.E. Wescon*, Pt. 7, Paper 11.4 (1963)
63. KEIDEL, W. D., 'Tuning Between Central Auditory Pathways and the Ear', *Trans. I.E.E.E.*, **Mil7**, 131 (1963)
64. VON BEKESY, G., 'Neural Funnelling Along the Skin and Between the Inner and Outer Hair Cells of the Cochlea', *J.A.S.A.*, **31**, 1236 (1959)
65. CALDWELL, W. D., 'Recognition of Sounds by Cochlea Patterns', *Trans. I.E.E.E.*, **Mil7**, 179 (1963)
66. MARTIN, T. B., and TALAVAGE, J. J., 'Application of Neural Logic to Speech Analysis and Recognition', *Trans. I.E.E.E.*, **Mil7**, 189 (1963)
67. STEWART, J. L., 'Fundamental Laws for Discrimination and Recognition in Animal Sensory Systems', *I.E.E.E. Conv. Record*, **11** (9), 158 (1963)
68. STEWART, J. L., 'Limits to Animal Discrimination and Recognition in a Noise-Free External Environment', *Trans. I.E.E.E.*, **Mil7**, 116 (1963)
69. SUZUKI, H., and OIZUMI, J., 'Binary Coding for Recognition: Learning of Japanese Vowels', *Electr. Commun. Japan*, **46**, 10 (1963)
70. SUZUKI, H., and OIZUMI, J., 'Vowel Discrimination by Means of Linear Discriminant Functions', *Electr. Commun. Japan*, **47**, 20 (1964)
71. HILLIX, W. A., 'Use of Two Non-Acoustic Measures in Computer Recognition of Spoken Digits', *J.A.S.A.*, **35**, 1978 (1963)
72. MAEZONO, K., 'Autocorrelation-Type Pitch Extractor', *Electr. Commun. Japan*, **46**, 10 (1963)
73. SAKAI, T., and DOSHITA, S., 'Speech-Recognition System for Conversational Sounds', *Electr. Commun. Japan*, **46**, 268 (1963)
74. SAKAI, T., and DOSHITA, S., 'The Automatic Speech Recognition System for Conversational Sound', *Trans. I.E.E.E.*, **EC12**, 835 (1963)
75. KATO, Y., *et al.*, 'Spoken Digit Recogniser', *Electr. Commun. Japan*, **47**, 31 (1964)
76. YOUNG, J. F., Electronic Learning Machine, British Patent Application 30657/68. Sponsored by N.R.D.C.

14

Past and Future

It will be seen that the time is ripe for an attempt to take a calm and unprejudiced look at where we are heading in cybernetics. For example, it is noticeable that in this sphere there has been an undue emphasis on the achievement by machines of accuracies of recognition undreamt of by mere erring humans. Is absolute accuracy really a measure of what we are seeking? Certainly it is for some machines of commercial application, but if the object is to press on and to find out how to simulate biological activity, accuracy is not the right target. Cybernetic work has been so varied that it is rash to generalise, but it would seem that there has been an undue concentration on learning and remembering and not enough on forgetting processes. The latter ability is an essential in any machine which is to be adaptable to changes in itself and in its environment. The difficulty lies in the problem of how to measure adaptability. It is the same difficulty which we have in measuring intelligence in human or in animal behaviour.

The theory of automata seems to be of little relevance to cybernetics as defined by Wiener. Toys and game-playing machines will probably be looked back on by later generations with the same gentle amusement we now bestow on von Kempelen's trick chess-player. On the other hand, some of the special-purpose machines are meeting a real need. There is likely to be particular interest in adaptive servo-systems if ever they can be produced economically. Work on visual pattern-recognition will certainly continue, though it is likely to become even more concentrated on avoidance of error rather than on adaptability to new situations. Pattern recognition is therefore likely to deviate more and more from biology. Fein[1] gives an amusing picture of the present position in cybernetics in the form of imaginary replies to an enquiry, as they would be written by various organisations. More recently (see Maxfield[2])

he has stimulated discussion by questioning the utility of digital computer stimulation and of neural net models in cybernetics.

Speech recognition involves one dimension less than visual pattern-recognition, though the variation in time is more rapid. To some extent, work on speech recognition is moving in the same direction as visual pattern-recognition, with the emphasis on freedom from error. Once again, while this is a commendable engineering aim, it is not really cybernetics. In the animal, occasional errors of control are essential if changing situations are to be handled. Some experimental learning machines have had this capability of adaptation, but it has been little emphasised in comparison with freedom from error.

Starting from the sort of work which has been presented earlier, an attempt will be made to distil the essential points and hence to postulate machines which display at least the fundamental characteristics of animal behaviour. We need not accept the statement of Descartes that it is morally impossible that there should be sufficient diversity in any machine to allow it to act in all the events of life in the same way as our reason causes us to act. In these days, the word 'impossible' is always taken rather as a challenge. However, we must retain a healthy scepticism about the possibilities of machines. Even if we enjoy reading science-fiction, we must be careful not to let ourselves be carried away in a flight of excessive imagination when discussing cybernetics. 'Knowledge is proud that he has learn'd so much, Wisdom is humble that he knows no more;' Cowper's warning is especially relevant to cybernetics investigators.

First, mere unpredictability is not enough. Predictability is a relative idea. Something can obey perfectly straightforward natural laws and yet be so complex that it is extremely difficult to predict its future. We have only to consider the English weather to see this. Even happenings on a much smaller scale, for example turbulence in a water jet, can be so complex as to be unpredictable. On the other hand, the behaviour of the simpler organisms is often remarkably predictable. The behaviour of some of the toys which have been built is complex but none the less predictable even though prediction would be difficult. As we study things having more and more possibilities of interaction between parts, prediction of future actions becomes so difficult that it is sensible to abandon any attempt to predict and to drop the consideration of predictability from our study.

Secondly, we must accept that although studies of assemblies of artificial nerve cells are interesting, such studies are unlikely to lead far for two reasons. In the first place, if we consider the number of

cells in the human brain, some 10,000 million of them, it will be seen that it is quite impractical even to approach such complexity in a machine at our present stage of knowledge. In the second place, most humans have difficulty in thinking of any extensive array of objects in three dimensions and studies of arrays of cells have usually been in two dimensions only. The number 10,000 million may be difficult to grasp. If the cells in a human brain were counted at a rate of one every second, day and night, it would take some 300 years, say from the time of Descartes until today. We must not expect to achieve such complexity with our present crude engineering techniques, although these crude techniques might help us towards an understanding of the operation of such a vast assembly of cells. It would certainly be interesting to investigate the behaviour of numbers of interconnected relaxation oscillators, each using several bi-stable elements in series, when some of the elements were caused to conduct prematurely by external inputs.

If direct simulation of the brain and central nervous system is not practicable, is it possible that instead we can imitate at least some of its behaviour patterns? It is useful here to make the distinction between molecular activity, i.e. processes actually proceeding within an organism, and molar activities, i.e. the behaviour of the organism in its environment. At the present stage of human knowledge, molar simulation of nervous activity is the more practicable. The outstanding feature which must be imitated is association, the conditioning both of reflexes and of inhibitions. It can be assumed that a large number of sensory inputs would be required and a large number of motor and inhibitor outputs. The sensory inputs and the motor outputs will be connected in a number of reflex and inhibitory arcs, and there will also be provision for the possibility of conditioning of the reflexes and inhibitions.

In a machine, it is not essential that the analogies of muscles and the reflexes and inhibitions be designed to aid the survival of the machine, but the action of the machine can nevertheless be regarded as homeostatic. In the living organism, the homeostasis is directed at survival. In the machine, homeostasis would simply be directed at maintaining constant some aspect of the machine operation. If we accept the hypothesis that the homeostasis of organisms is directed mainly to the removal of disturbing inputs, then the homeostasis of an analogous machine should also be directed to this end. The machine must be capable of remembering associations in order that it can retain conditioned reflexes. It is equally important that the machine be capable of forgetting associations. The term 'forgetting' means that older associations which are not reinforced reasonably frequently shall become less and less important com-

pared with recently acquired associations. It is not required that old associations should be erased completely, only that they shall be rendered less capable of evoking a response and therefore less important.

The whole of the memory process should be based on probability. If a certain sensory input is associated frequently with another input which is connected with a particular reflex arc, then there is a high probability that the two inputs will again be associated in the future. If the joint occurrence has not happened for a long time, then the probability of the happening decreases. The longer the interval since the last joint occurrence of the two inputs, the lower the probability of their joint occurrence in the future. Thus, in order for the machine to be able to use its memory of associations, the memory should be reinforced each time that the association occurs and the memory should decay, say exponentially, with time if it is not reinforced. The memory will then never decay to zero but as time goes on without reinforcement the memory will become less and less important. In this way the machine can adapt its actions to changes in its environment.

The main feedback path for the animal process of homeostasis is via the external environment. There are, however, local internal feedback paths for various special functions. The action of the autonomic nervous system is an example where feedback is almost entirely internal. Internal feedback is important in a machine firstly to reduce the accuracy requirements in its control mechanisms. By using feedback as in a servo-system and by controlling muscles according to the error in the desired result, i.e. according to the difference between the actual result and the desired result of an action, it is not necessary to have precise and unvarying relationships between, for example, the nerve impulses coming to a muscle and the actual resulting muscle movement. Even though the relationship varies, feedback can ensure that the accuracy of control is not seriously impaired. The second reason for the use of internal feedback in the nervous system or in the machine is to allow internal inhibition to operate. Internal inhibition can prevent the organism or the machine from operating on the environment until an opportune moment arrives, that is, until the positive, excitatory, inputs are sufficiently strong to overcome the negative, inhibitory, inputs which are preventing the operation. It is tempting to regard such a process of inhibition as abstract thought, but that would be venturing too far beyond the bounds of available evidence.

To stimulate a nervous system, a machine must be able to recognise patterns. This includes not only visually discernible

patterns but also patterns of sound, touch, heat, etc. and patterns formed from combinations of various different stimuli. Patterns could be recognised and used to initiate actions by a mere extension of the process of association to the correlation of many different inputs. However, recent work in physiology has made it seem likely that there is, in some cases at least, an enhancement of contrast in the sensory nerves which aids the recognition of patterns. Consider a typical visual pattern, common enough in England, a red L on a white background. Most of the area of the sign conveys little if any information to us at all. It is the configuration of the junction between red and white which really enables us to know that this is an L and not a T. Consequently it would be a waste of the facilities of the central nervous system if the information about the blank background and the blank part inside the boundaries of the L was not ignored. It is the contrast between the red L and the white background which is important in perceiving the pattern. Certain nerve cells apparently enhance contrast by mutual inhibition, and it would be desirable if a simulating machine could have such facilities also.

Most sensory nerve cells have the property of adaptation. When their excitation varies, they give a burst of activity which gradually dies away. This has the effect of enhancing the contrast between 'activity' and 'no activity'. The effect is similar to the so-called quasi-differential effect easily obtained with electrical circuits. It would therefore not be too difficult to build such effects into a simulating machine, though it would certainly add to the complication of such a machine if very many sensory elements were involved. Another desirable feature in a simulating machine is that the sensory elements should obey something like the Fechner–Weber law. This would have the effect of enabling the sensory elements to operate over a wide range of degrees of stimulation without saturation.

Let us consider the sort of behaviour which would be expected of a machine built to meet the sort of specification which has been derived above. Assume that some of the sensory inputs come from a microphone and others from a keyboard having several numbered buttons. The buttons are connected into various reflex arcs controlling lamps, so that every time the button marked '1' is pressed, a corresponding lamp marked '1' lights. Now if the machine is capable of associating the coincidence of various inputs, we can say 'one' into the microphone each time that we press the button marked '1'. Eventually when the sound of the word 'one' has coincided with the pressing of the button a number of times, the memory units of the machine will have recorded that this is a very probable association. If now we simply say 'one' into the micro-

phone, there is a good chance that the corresponding lamp will light even though we do not press the button marked '1'. In other words, we expect the machine to learn to recognise the spoken word 'one' and to have a good probability of acting accordingly.

It is important to note that the machine is not expected to learn to carry out certain actions infallibly in response to certain stimuli. This is not a characteristic of the conditioning process. The probability of carrying out certain actions in response to certain stimuli is increased by conditioning, but infallibility is a property only of some reflex arcs and not of conditioned reflexes. The saying 'to err is human' appears to be a basic principle of physiology. The more often the conditioning process is repeated, the greater the probability that the corresponding action will be carried out. However, the longer the interval since the last occurrence of a particular conditioning process, the lower is the probability that the corresponding action will be carried out. To express this in everyday language, recent events are remembered more easily than events which occurred earlier. The possibility of erring increases with the time since the last reinforcement of a conditioned reflex. Pavlov's team observed a forgetting or extinction effect in their experimental animals. From all the observed facts Pavlov came to the conclusion that the extinction of conditioned reflexes which were not reinforced was due to an inhibitory process. The conditioned reflex which has been subject to deliberate extinction is not destroyed, in fact it recovers in time. This is not the process which we really mean when we use the term 'forgetting'. It seems to be natural, following human experience, to assume that unreinforced memory merely decays with time. Certainly, Walter and other makers of machines seem to have accepted this without question. The present writer has found it difficult to discover verifying documentation on animal experiments concerned specifically with the natural forgetting process, but this might well be due to not looking in the correct place. If not, there is a curious omission in the literature (however, see Underwood[3]).

In the circumstances, it can be postulated that memories do decay, and that they decay approximately exponentially with time if they are not reinforced. It can be assumed that such a process of forgetting is a desirable feature in a machine intended to simulate the action of the central nervous system. Such a process will prevent the memory store from becoming overloaded with redundant information.

Sklansky has suggested that feedback is not a necessary feature of a learning process. However, essentially, a machine with a well-defined aim can train itself to achieve the aim by using feedback, even if the inputs are completely random. This is the advantage to be gained from the deliberate use of homeostasis. In effect, the

inputs and the actions are associated with achievement or non-achievement of the aim.

A simple associating machine can be trained by a human operator who, in the process of making adjustments, carries out deliberate feedback. An aimless associating machine can achieve completely error-free association provided that the nature of the inputs does not change. However, without any form of feedback, changes of environment must introduce ambiguity in the actions of the machine. The ambiguity can be made less important by a forgetting process, but inevitably the machine can then no longer be error-free. Completely random inputs to a non-feedback associating machine are meaningless and cannot be used in the learning process. It is interesting to note that the teaching-machine approach of Skinner can be compared with that of Crowder in a similar way.

REFERENCES

1. FEIN, L., 'The Artificial Intelligentsia', *I.E.E.E. Wescon*, Pt. 7, Paper 11.1 (1963)
2. MAXFIELD, M., *et al.*, *Biophysics and Cybernetic Systems*, Macmillan (1965)
3. UNDERWOOD, B. J., 'Forgetting', *Sc. Amer.*, **210**, 91 (1964)

15

The Designer's Dilemma

From the available experimental evidence on animals and man, there seems to be a definite relationship between intelligence and inhibition, even allowing for difficulties in defining the former. Higher animals have a richer opportunity for inhibition in the central nervous system than have lower animals. Kohler showed that in an attempt to obtain food, monkeys had no difficulty in first moving directly away from the food in order to pass an obstacle. Hens, on the other hand, seemed unable to inhibit their instinctive movement towards food despite an obstacle which could only be passed by first moving away from the food. Pavlov quarrelled with Kohler's conclusions but agreed with the experimental results. The particular point of difference was the question of what an ape is doing when it just sits down and looks at a problem. Kohler said 'thinking', Pavlov said 'resting'. Let us sidetrack the argument, since the only way really to discover the answer would be to ask an ape.

What would be lost if intelligence was defined simply as 'a capacity for inhibition'? Such a definition might not accord with some of the work of psychologists (though, as mentioned in Chapter 4, Thurstone proposed this as early as 1924). For example, the definition seems to have little direct relationship to I.Q. tests. However, a little thought shows that this definition can even have a relationship to such activities as intelligence testing. If one thinks of some aspect of intelligent human activity, i.e. that sort of activity which we regard as intelligent, it is always found that such activity involves the inhibition or postponement of some natural instinctive action. When faced with a surfeit of food, only the unintelligent eats until he is overfull. An intelligent person eats enough and no more. A less intelligent person is unable to save money in order to buy something expensive, while a more intelligent person considers the future and

not only the present. All intelligent human activity can be considered from this point of view, and the same trends can be seen in intelligent animal activity. Without inhibition there could be no civilisation. In fact, without inhibition there could not even be any animal herds.

It is possible to become really controversial by suggesting that thought itself is the process carried out when instinctive activity is inhibited. As long as the inhibition is effective, various sensory inputs and memories are present. These inputs and memories form the data on which the inhibition is based, the inhibition being produced by conditioned association of various inputs and memories. The inhibition is only released when there appears a sufficient number of excitatory inputs to counterbalance the inhibitory influences. Such a hypothesis can be elaborated, but this will not be attempted here since it has not sufficient significance to the main argument.

Another controversial point is the possible capacity of any machine to appreciate a concept such as 'blueness'. This point is often raised in verbal arguments and occasionally in the technical press. For example, Tustin has raised the point when reviewing one of Wiener's books. The difficulty which Tustin sees is that blueness is an experience and as such it is outside the vocabulary of physics. The point is applicable also to thought, since this is another personal experience. The only way we have, at present, of comparing personal experiences is by communication in some other form. For example, we can give a colour a verbal name such as 'red'. This enables us to determine when a person or an animal is incapable of appreciating certain colours, since we can compare the response to two different named colours. In this way we can discover that most mammals except monkeys are colour-blind and we can also discover that a truly colour-blind person sees all colours just as if they were shades of grey. Naming colours also enables us to compare colours with scientific measurements, for example with wavelength measurements. However, while you and I might agree that a particular tomato is red, there can be no guarantee that our subjective experiences are the same. For all I know, your subjective experience of red might be the same as my subjective experience of green, but even so, as long as we agree on a name for the colour all is well and there is no confusion. A person born blind who gains sight for the first time when adult, sees a dancing pattern of colour and at first has difficulty in making a colour (or a shape) 'stick' to an observed object. It is necessary to learn to see colours and shapes for oneself. Tustin feels that there is room for an enlargement of physics into what might be called psycho-physics. All we need consider here is that if ever we get to the point where a machine agrees with us that an object is red, and then it tells us that it experiences redness, we

shall have no alternative but to believe it. At least such tests are not impossible, even if we do not yet know how to carry them out, and we are not eternally condemned to pure faith in our beliefs as far as subjective experience is concerned.

The designer of machines intended to simulate nervous activity is almost inevitably drawn into some philosophising about his own activity. This is because he cannot be quite certain about what to design until he has actually built something and tried it out. In some scientific work it is possible to carry out much of the research on paper in the form of calculations. The conclusions reached from the calculations can then be tested by experiment. The designer of machines of the type discussed here is in a less fortunate position. It is not too difficult to produce a bookful of pseudo-mathematics which is of virtually no use to a would-be designer. The designer, instead of carrying out paper experiments in search of a meaningful pattern, has to examine physiology and behaviour in the hope of simplifying the data (while not over-simplifying) and recognising here patterns which will lead to useful generalisations. Some of this sort of work has been discussed in the critical review given earlier. Some of it has been given in the form of a rough machine specifiction. It is not pretended that the generalisations are entirely coherent. However, they show signs of leading to a machine which will be more than a toy.

Suppose we built a machine which really does simulate nervous activity and which could be taught to do a useful job. It would have a capacity for conditioning, both of its reflexes and of its inhibitions. It would have a memory and a 'forgettory' and it would operate on probabilities. It would therefore be fallible. We are left with a nagging thought. For what reason would the machine carry out all of these activities? There must be some object in view if the activity is to be purposeful and not merely random. Is it sufficient to design the machine to remove disturbing sensory inputs? Let us return to the organism for a guide to our answer. Why does an organism behave as it does? The generally accepted answer here is homeostasis. The organism behaves as it does because it is alive and the characteristic of life is homeostasis. The organism must interchange with its surroundings and yet remain differentiated from its surroundings in order to survive. The object of the organism's behaviour, of its entire behaviour, is survival of the individual and of the species. Such an object is completely selfish, without a trace of true altruism.

Such entirely selfish behaviour is all we find in many creatures, particularly the lower, less intelligent, creatures. However, Kropotkin has pointed out that animals which display the greatest degree of pure selfishness do not always come out best in the struggle

for survival. Animals which display highly developed herd activity and which work together for mutual attack or defence have an improved chance of survival. Co-operation within a species is more effective than competition. Kropotkin regards herd activity as altruism. It is equally possible to regard it as sensible selfishness. The animal uses its intelligence and inhibits its natural desires more or less because by so doing it improves its chances of survival. Observation of the life of, say, a tribe of baboons shows that there is little or no evidence of true altruism. Fox has pointed out the existence of harsh social distinctions and real natural selfishness within a group, the social distinctions leading to fights in which one male is deposed by another. It seems that in Nature there are at least two forms of selfishness; primitive selfishness, which we might call stupid selfishness, and the more advanced and effective form which we can call sensible selfishness. We do not need to postulate the existence of altruism at all.

Can this point of view be extended to human behaviour? Here we immediately run into trouble from the various religious faiths and from some non-religious philosophies. It seems that, although the facts of evolution are generally accepted today, there is a widespread acceptance of a sudden change of a different nature when the evolution of man is considered. The fact of man's vastly improved means of communication is obvious, and this is probably the most important factor which has led to civilisation. We can guess that the brain of man has evolved in the direction of increased possibility for inhibition. For many, such a view is not enough. Man has a mind, they say, animals have none. Now this is a most curious piece of evolution to accept. The other two points, communication and inhibition, were truly evolutionary in that they were improved versions of what had gone before. But this sudden appearance of 'mind', if we accept it, is a completely new phenomenon and it does not fit in with the usually accepted pattern of evolution, since we are told that earlier creatures did not even have a crude form of mind.

This difficulty dates back at least to Descartes, who even assumed that there was a definite point in the brain through which it was controlled by the mind. Such a dualism has obtained such a firm hold on popular opinion that it is even subscribed to by some leading scientists working on problems of the nervous system. For example, Sherrington once said that the physical basis of mind encroaches more and more upon the study of mind, but there remain mental events which seem to be beyond any physiology of the brain. There are many scientists even now who cling to the view of Descartes. If we examine their views and, as usual, look for an underlying pattern, it seems possible that it is not so much the possession

of an inanimate mind which is important to them as the possession of free will. There seems to be an underlying fear that without an inanimate mind there can be no free will, that all of one's actions are predetermined by the very structure of the nervous system and the environment of the body. Basically, it seems that this attitude is that there must be no danger that one carries out evil actions simply because one cannot help doing so. This attitude is difficult to understand in scientific terms.

It must be difficult for those who believe in the duality of mind and brain to maintain their position in the light of knowledge gained by modern brain surgery. There is no doubt that the personality can be changed by brain surgery, and it can be changed in the direction of reduction of inhibition, which is not always a good thing. A dualist must therefore accept that surgery of the brain can affect the inanimate mind. It should be mentioned that some eminent brain surgeons do manage to accept dualism.

Suppose that we accept, at least tentatively, the idea that the human brain is evolved directly from the animal brain. Suppose that we accept that the great leap forward lies solely in the elaboration of facilities for inhibition and communication. These two features are of course closely interlinked. The fundamental objective of the human organism is homeostasis. Its actions are ultimately intended to promote survival of itself and of the species. The human being is, therefore, basically a selfish creature, interested primarily in its own survival. In pursuing this course, the creature finds it advantageous to live in tribes. This is merely an example of the application of inhibition and communication. There is no true altruism, there is nothing but selfishness.

This is a shocking concept to those who have some faith in metaphysics. In fact, it is a rather worrying concept for the machine designer. Is the successful machine designer destined to be a Frankenstein? Can we look forward, as did Capek, to the day when robots will rise in revolt against the human race? The designer turns from the future to the present-day, and still his thoughts are flooded with troublesome questions. Is there no altruism? Is altruism aberration? Why do people behave as they do if all the evidence points to their drives being merely homeostasis? Perhaps here we can quote an unnamed, though eminent, philosopher who was asked by a third party to comment: '. . . some actions are more concerned with the preservation of the race, via the preservation of some other members of the race, than the preservation of the agent; and what else is altruism than that?'.

Homeostasis is a process of self-preservation. The organism makes every attempt to remove those sensory inputs which disturb the

basic pattern of its life. In the case of a human being, we say that he takes steps to remove sensory inputs which disturb his contentment. In the lowest forms of life, we find only reflex activity, but we have seen that conditioning and then inhibition is encountered higher up the evolutionary scale. An animal will inhibit its natural reaction to a tickling fly if the action of brushing away the fly is likely to disturb the prey of the animal and so prolong the major disturbance of hunger.

Animals which live in herds or tribes find that some inhibition is necessary in order to obtain the advantages of so doing. Such inhibition promotes the survival of the animal. We must not lose sight of the fact, however, that the main drive is individual survival. An animal living in a community finds that in its own interest it should inhibit some of its instinctive activity in favour of collective activity. The animal which fails to do so is in danger from other members of the community, and its contentment is short-lived. In order to achieve any real contentment, an animal must be surrounded by contentment. The sensible, intelligent animal will promote the contentment of others. By so doing it will in turn promote its own contentment. This will necessitate the inhibition of much of the animal's reflex activity, but such inhibition is essential to the survival of the animal in its environment.

This, then, is the hypothesis to which the designer comes. Make your machine homeostatic and you make your machine inherently selfish. It cannot be 'blamed' for this, such action is inherent in the way the machine is built. Allow the homeostatic process to include inhibition, and you give your machine the opportunity to display intelligent activity. The drive is homeostasis, the machine is inherently and incurably selfish. If little capacity for intelligent inhibition is built into the machine, its behaviour will be describable as stupid selfishness. On the other hand, if there is capacity for intelligent inhibition, and this capacity is used in the homeostatic process, we can describe the behaviour of the machine as sensible selfishness.

And at this point we abandon the subject. For from here on we enter the realms of philosophy and as always we must expect philosophy to take a long time, centuries even, before it can become reconciled to current scientific knowledge. Unfortunately, by the time philosophy is reconciled, the knowledge will no longer be current, and the struggle for reconciliation will go on. . . .

Index